No Apology Necessary,

Just Respect

Rev. Earl Carter

CREATION
HOUSE
Orlando, FL

No Apology Necessary, Just Respect by Rev. Earl Carter

Published by Creation House
Strang Communications Company
600 Rinehart Road, Lake Mary, Florida 32746
Web site: http://www.creationhouse.com

Unless otherwise noted, all Scripture quotations are from
the King James Version of the Bible.

Scripture quotations marked NKJV are from the
New King James Version of the Bible.
Copyright © 1979, 1980, 1982
by Thomas Nelson Inc., Publishers.
Used by permission.

Library of Congress Catalog Card Number: 96-71396
International Standard Book Number: 0-88419-455-8

89012345 BBG 8765432
Printed in the United States of America

SPECIAL ACKNOWLEDGMENT

To my splendid wife, Beverly, my Queen of the Nile, who challenged my message with objective reviews and helped me to maintain scriptural integrity. My first disciple of such a hard message.

To my dear babies Dominique and E. J., who sacrificed many hours of their "special time" together with their dad during the writing of this book.

CONTENTS

Introduction 7

1   My Black Experience 9

2   A New Start 13

3   The Origin of the Races 19

4   Ancient Powers — Egypt and Ethiopia 25

5   The Biblical Account of Slavery 35

6   Who Sent the Ships? 39

7   Prophecy Continued:
     The Black Man Today, Part I 49

8   Prophecy Continued:
     The Black Man Today, Part II 57

9   Christianity's Answer to Farrakhan . , , , ...65

10 The Healing of the Black Man 75

11 Prophecy Continued:
     The Irritated Heart of the White Man 83

12 The Healing of the White Man 91

13 Healing in the Church 95

14 No Apology Necessary, Just Respect 101

15 Coming Together 111

     Endnotes 116

     Suggested Reading 120

INTRODUCTION

No white man could write this book. It's dangerous enough for a black man to say these things, let alone a white man. This book is what I call *skandalizo* — it will offend you. It will offend your mind, your emotions, and your habits of thinking. But it will heal your heart. Let me tell you why.

The mindset of the black community has always thought we were in Africa, living peacefully and minding our own business with one another in a seemingly utopian environment, when the greedy and imperialistic whites came in ships to enslave us.

But now, in this day and hour, God is revealing the truth about slavery to His people. He is giving us understanding of the prophecies of Isaiah and Ezekiel so we can learn what really happened to the blacks — and why. The prophecies in these ancient books still affect the black race even as we exist today!

Recent events such as the Rodney King incident and the O.J. Simpson trial demonstrate the polarization of whites and blacks in this country. So to deny that we have racial problems in America is unrealistic and passive. Racial prejudice is still overtly perpetrated on blacks, and reverse racism is committed against whites.

And our country is crying out for an absolute answer to the problem. So is the church. This desire for reconciliation has led to a church movement that consists of whites apologizing to the blacks for slavery and all the atrocities committed against them. But is that really bringing healing and closure?

The only absolute answer comes from absolute truth. And the only place we find absolute truth is in the Bible.

The Truth — Can You Handle It?

Both whites and blacks are enslaved by the misinformation and the ignorance that promotes racism. Blacks are enslaved by anger, hatred, and blame, while whites are enslaved by guilt and irritated hearts.

This is why it is incumbent upon me to to articulate this truth so we might have healing and closure, because the truth in this book will set everyone free.

I have talked to some black clergy who say the white man is using the same things I declare in this book to justify his racism. But that is not accurate. This new revelation is different from the old story. Because most whites and blacks have not heard where their anger and irritated hearts truly came from.

A Ph. D. friend of mine advised me not to write a book like this because it would infuriate or even hurt the black people. But when I gave him the truth of my text, he could not successfully refute it.

Even at the risk of being perceived as a traitor or being exploited by those who would use this writing to justify slavery, I must tell the truth. Because the truth brings healing to everyone — to both sides.

But again, if you can't handle the truth, don't read this book. And if you choose to read it, don't read this book partially. Because unless you read the entire book, you won't get the full picture. As Solomon wrote, "It is not wise to answer a matter before it is heard in its entirety."

The truth in this book is like a bomb. It may explode inside you, as it did in me. But if you let it, the bomb will become a balm.

So please, read the truth and be healed, just as I was.

ONE

My Black Experience

———

It was a night like many other nights. My friends and I were standing on the corner drinking and just hanging out. We didn't have jobs, but we always looked good, and we liked the girls to see us.

We noticed two white men coming out of a nearby store. They shouldn't have come into our area. This was warfare — these white men were in the enemy's camp, and they were about to get what they deserved.

One of my friends, Cutler, ran right up to the men. He elbowed one over and knocked the other one to the ground with his fist. Then he began to kick and stomp them.

What had these men done wrong? They were white and alone. My friends and I always used to take advantage of that situation. They weren't the first white men we had accosted, and they wouldn't be the last. We preyed on white men whenever we could.

After the first blows, my friends and I ran over to join in. I looked on, laughing at the scene because we all felt like we were getting even. We felt justified in our violence toward whites because of slavery. But Cutler was over the edge...he was consumed by rage.

"Take your shoes off," Cutler screamed at them. He always liked to make them leave barefooted. But as he shouted, the store owner, a Jewish man, rushed out with the biggest gun I had ever seen and began shooting at us wildly, so we fled into an alley. I will never forget

9

sprinting through that narrow alley that was lit up with gunfire, and how we narrowly escaped. Because it was that night that I realized I could have been killed—all because of my anger at the white man.

The Quest for Revenge

In Charleston, South Carolina, where I grew up, the artifacts of slavery can still be seen. Down on the waterfront there is a park called the Battery where an old slave market used to be. Now visitors can peer into its holding cells where slaves waited until they were brought up to the platform to be auctioned off. I remember going there with my family when I was a a child. We would look at that old slave market and wonder, *Why did that have to happen to us as a people?* And I remember thinking that one day—I would get revenge.

As a youth, I tried to get that revenge in many ways. We had black movie theaters in Charleston, so we usually went to those. But there was one white theater downtown that would let blacks sit up in the balcony. It was really stupid to allow us up there because God knows the things we did. We would take vengeance on the white people sitting below us by throwing sodas and ice on them—and that wasn't the worst of it. We used to do some terrible things, even to the point of almost throwing somebody over the balcony.

In the early '60s there was a civil rights march in Charleston during which the police chief was hit in the head with a brick. I was one of those in the crowd throwing them. I didn't know exactly why I was doing it. I was twelve or thirteen years old and simply caught up in the mob.

When the chief of police came up bleeding, we applauded each other. Today we would give each other the high five. But back then we congratulated each other by raising a fist, the black Power symbol.

Street Life

As I grew into my teens I hardened even more. Between the ages of twelve and sixteen I was arrested at least seven times for breaking in, beating up people, and robbing stores. We used to tie a rag around a sledge hammer, break through a store's wall, then roll the safe out. My friends and I used to also regularly break into the dairy to steal eggs and bacon to sell them to local stores. Everyone knew they were black market, but that's how we made our money.

10

We were precocious young men who wore expensive clothes. Looking good was important because it brought respect, so we went to Fathers and Sons, a popular clothing store, and stole from them to look street good. When we went to parties, the girls would notice. And that was important, because that was our world. Fighting and looking sharp for the girls—that's all we had and all we cared about.

I could never bring myself to be too brutal unless a white man called me, "Boy." Anyone who made that mistake had to back down, or we could fight to the end because respect was very important to me. My brother and friends had no mercy regardless of the situation. One night they broke into a pawn shop and stole some guns. But we never got the chance to use them, to my relief, because I constantly tried to keep the guys from killing anybody to keep myself out of the electric chair. It should suffice to say, though, that we were a pretty tough group.

No Honor Among Thieves

Once I worked for a lady who had a filling station right across the street from my house. She didn't know that we'd already broken into every place around the neighborhood except hers, so she hired me to pump gas and clean up.

Well, one night my friends and I were on the corner with nothing to do when they spotted a television in her filling station and said, "Hey, man, we haven't broken into that place yet." I protested, saying that it was my place of employment, but they talked me into it. So we broke into the place, stole the television and hid it under my house.

A few days later I was trying to impress a girl while walking home from school, acting cool, when two detectives drove up alongside us.

"All right, Carter, let's go. Get in the car," said one of the detectives.

"No, man, what you want me for?" I responded defensively.

Someone had squealed on me about the television, and all of the sudden these cops were jerking me up by the seat of my pants while pushing me along painfully on my tip-toes to their car. The young lady ran away. I felt so embarrassed.

While in jail, I remember wondering whether this was all there was to life—feeling boxed in and hopeless. I didn't know what to do or where to turn, so I kept on being angry at society and the white man in general. He was the cause of it all, I determined, so I hated him and all he represented.

Home Life

My mother and father were separated when I was just starting elementary school, and I honestly don't remember ever being a child. The sort of carefree young life many children live never transpired in me. I was a very precocious young man who ripened before his time. My four brothers, sister, and I lived with my father, but we were left to ourselves most of the time because he was constantly at work. My mother would visit us occasionally, but because she didn't get along with my father at all and was constantly ill, her visits were very rare.

So my brother and I got kicked out of several schools and most of our friends were criminals. Some of them were shot to death. Others died trying to escape from prison. Cutler was killed by a bartender. They died in the problem, complete slaves to their hate and anger, in poverty and hopelessness. But somehow, Jesus got a hold of me.

TWO

A New Start

I hitchhiked out of Charleston in 1965 when I was almost sixteen to live with my aunt in Philadelphia because I didn't want to be a recidivist—one who relapses back into the same problems. I wanted to change. I believe my mother's suffering kept me sensitive to God during that time because of all the prayers I offered in the hopes of her getting well.

When I was almost seventeen I was coming out of a bar and walked right into a street meeting a local church was holding. I was a little drunk, but I listened because I had respect for religious people. After listening a while, a young man came up and told me about Jesus. I gave him my address and must have agreed to go to church with him, because bright and early Sunday morning, he showed up at my door.

I had been partying again the night before. In fact, I was blessed to be alive. I had been in a couple bad fights, and I certainly didn't remember accepting an invitation to church. So I tried to get rid of this persistent fellow. But he kept reminding me of how I agreed to come with him to church on Sunday, and that appealed to the little integrity I had, so I said okay. I did, however, get ready as slowly as I could, just to annoy him.

When we arrived at the service, the church people were nice, but I was mean. I didn't want anything to do with them, so I sat in the back. When they invited me to sit up front, I coldly said, "No, I'm not going to be here long." I was really irritated.

Then the choir sang and some people started dancing. I thought they looked so funny that I shoved my head down behind the pew and laughed. But I couldn't help noticing that there was something about these people which was very different. They really got my attention.

I understood some of the things the preacher said about God loving us and wanting to bring us into a new life. But more powerful than what he said was what I saw — young men and women like myself who were converted. I could relate to one guy in particular because he reminded me of myself from the street. I recognized that he was once out there, so I kept my eyes on him.

If God can do something for that guy, maybe He can do something for me, I said to myself. But then I thought, *Aw, that's just for him.* Yet, when the altar call was given, I heard a voice within me say, *Why don't you give Me a chance? If you would let Me come in your heart, I'll make your life beautiful.*

I couldn't resist, so I said, "Well, Lord, if this is You, I'm going to try it," and I got up. I felt like a hundred pounds of weight was strapped to each foot. I struggled to walk down that aisle, but I kept on trudging. I finally made it to the altar and gave my heart to the Lord.

I'm so glad Jesus works from the bottom up, because I was certainly on the bottom!

When I got home that night, I felt a freedom that I had never felt before. Over the next few weeks, I tried to drink and smoke again, but those things just made me uncomfortable. I always threw the cigarettes away.

No Pleasure in Sin Anymore

After a couple of years had passed I went back to drinking and partying for a while, but I was miserable. I'd be drinking and crying in my beer. I had to be drunk to go to sleep because I felt so guilty. I did anything to drown out my consciousness of God, but nothing worked. I couldn't enjoy sin. I felt hurt that I left Jesus, but I had been convinced that I wasn't worthy to go back to Him. Jesus had been so good to me, and there I was, out there acting stupid, smoking cigarettes, partying, running around with women again — and I couldn't even enjoy myself. Plus, I felt bad because I had told some people about Jesus, and there I was a misfit again.

Then one night in a vision I saw blood all over the city. I felt like it was the blood of innocent souls who would be lost because of my lack of obedience to God — people I wouldn't reach whose blood would be required at my hand. That woke me up spiritually, so I went back to the church and got reclaimed.

Saved, but Still Angry

As I committed my life and grew in the faith, I joined the Church of God in Christ. In 1969 I became a Church of God in Christ minister. But I still had anger for the so-called oppressor — the white man — festering in me. I was glad to be in a black denomination with black leaders, because I didn't want any white man to lead me. I felt safe and secure in the black church.

I ran into a white minister on a number or occasions who seemed to be prejudiced against black ministry, against the Afrocentric style. He wanted to do things the Eurocentric way only. And he ran into a problem when he ran into me. I didn't want anything to do with white ministries — period. And I told everyone how I felt. After a while I was overseeing a personal crusade to bring an awareness of the disparity between the white and black church. The prosperity of the white church and the poverty of the black church that I saw led me to believe the whites were suppressing the blacks. So I felt obligated to expose covert racism. It even got to the point that if I saw whites in the congregation when I was preaching, I took the opportunity to vent my feelings about racism.

In 1976 I became preoccupied with what was happening in South Africa. Apartheid dominated the news. Even though racial tension in the United States had subsided some, I saw a reflection of what was happening in South Africa, in America. Seeing the violence on television struck a nerve. So I began a relentless quest to find a reason for racism. Why were we treated so badly as a people?

Preaching Anger and Resentment

It is no secret that the black pulpit in America is often used to advance social issues because blacks are the ones with the social struggle. Whites don't have that struggle. So I preached strongly about racism, about the atrocities and injustices of apartheid. But I had some misinformation and half-truths. I thought like everybody else in the black community — that the whites were perpetrating racism because of their imperialistic attitude...their greed and feelings of superiority.

The goal of my preaching was to make white people feel guilty enough to pay for what they did. And for black people to understand the struggle wasn't over, so they would fight for justice.

I preached that we black people were going to be justified one day. And I went into a lot of historical detail concerning our history of slavery, the slave ships, and the terrible conditions slaves faced. I could preach all day on the black man's oppression. And when I was finished, any white people within ear-shot were ready to get up and run out, and the black people who heard me were ready to fight. I felt like God was on our side, and that He would lead us out of our discrimination and injustice. But reconciliation was the farthest thing from my mind, so I stayed in the safe haven of the Church of God in Christ.

One service in which I was preaching this message to a mixed congregation, I took notice of the faces of some white people who were listening, and saw that they were really hurt. It was almost as if they were saying, "If we had been there, we wouldn't have done those things." I often made the congregations feel bad because I was still angry. I cried a lot because I couldn't resort to violence like I used to and the anger of all our injustices still burned deep inside. But not long after that service, God told me to stop using His pulpit to deliver anger, so I quit for many years.

Then, in 1994, I preached a variation of the message as a guest speaker at a series of meetings in Ft. Lauderdale, Florida. I talked about how slavery affected the black man and his ability to form relationships with his wife and family. I also concentrated on the psychological effects of slavery — how it had paralyzed the black man and affected his whole existence. And, of course, I blamed the white man.

After one meeting a black lady sent me a note telling me that some of her best friends were white, and that they weren't hateful or prejudiced. And she questioned why I hated white people so much. At first I brushed it off. I figured she was brainwashed because she had white friends, and that she must have felt the struggle was over...because it was over for her. I believed she had simply excused herself from it.

But when many other blacks were so upset that they didn't return to my meetings, I finally woke up to what I was actually doing. Now I had received negative responses from both blacks and whites, and that made me realize something really was wrong in me. I knew I was a Christian, but I also knew something was wrong inside.

I was preaching "some" truth, but I didn't have the whole picture. Then in 1995 when I was preaching a message at home on the restoration of the black man, one of my members said to me after the service, "Pastor, I know why we ended up in slavery." I couldn't imagine what she knew, but my interest was raised. "Tell me," I said. In response she gave me a book, *Bible Legacy of the Black Race* by Joyce Andrews. The book was based on certain Bible prophecies as they relate to the black man today. And when I started reading it, the missing pieces of my puzzle began to fall into place.

Because He Loves Us

Then during an airline flight to a speaking engagement in California later that year, I picked up a copy of the airline magazine that contained the carrier's flight routes all over the world. As I looked at the west coast of Africa and at the vast Atlantic ocean the slave ships had to cross, I remembered the many books I had read about the terrible conditions my ancestral Africans had to suffer. Those who died during the journey were thrown to the sharks that followed the ships. The sick and diseased died in their own filth and vomit. Others tried to kill themselves in gruesome ways, even by starving to death.

I was angry at the white people for being the slave masters, at black people for being the slaves, and I didn't know how to deal with my feelings.

"Why, God?" I moaned quietly in that airplane seat. I had been mulling over in my mind Joyce Andrews book, so I asked as I had never asked before, because I had to know: "Why did this have to happen to us?"

Then God spoke to my heart right there at 30,000 feet. Now this may shock some of you — but the Lord told me slavery happened because He loved us so much. He showed me the same truth that day I am now sharing with you in this book. I started crying right there on the airplane, because I finally understood. I saw that it was ALL in the prophecies — not only the slavery, but the reason blacks are the way we are today as well as the conditions we face. I finally had the whole picture.

Truth Set Me Free

So over the next few months I read and researched a lot. And the more I learned, the more excited I became. Discovering my black history gave me strength. I finally knew my own identity, and I knew the white man's role in history. It all made sense at last. And best of all, I was set free from resentment and rage I had carried all my life. I had been a resentful Christian for almost thirty years. But all that vanished, because the truth set me free from the fury. I had been so saturated in the world's thinking about slavery and the condition of blacks, that I didn't know there was any other way to think. But when I saw it God's way, I was changed from the inside out. His truth set me free.

Are you white, and do you feel blamed for something you didn't do? Or are you black and angry because of the opportunities you haven't had? If you are either, you need to know that God wants to set you free — with His truth.

To uncover the truth, we have to go back in time to the ancient black civilizations — the nations that came from Noah's son Ham. Ham's sons — Canaan, Mizraim, Cush and Phut — aren't just odd names of people who died long ago. They are nations that exist today, people from whom the blacks in America today directly descended. In the next chapter we will find out who they were, and what God prophesied about them.

THREE

The Origin of the Races

———

In his book, *Roots*, Alex Haley gives a wonderful depiction of the origins of his family. But he doesn't go back far enough to tell the whole story of the black race, because Mr. Haley's book begins in the bush lands, and the black race and its many variations were around long before that.

The ancient civilizations of Ethiopia, Egypt, and others in Africa, were founded by the black sons of Ham. So our origin is not in the African bush, but in the pageantry and grandeur of ancient Egypt and its sister, Ethiopia.

The Beginnings of the Nations

You will read in Genesis 10 that Noah's three sons, Shem, Ham and Japheth, were the progenitors of the nations. And that through them and their descendants, all the nations of the world were established. From the descendants of Japheth came the Greeks, the Romans, the Germans and the Russians. So the descendants of Japheth are considered to be the progenitors of the white, or Caucasian race, that migrated up into the northern areas of Europe and Asia.

Ham's descendants populated Canaan, Egypt, Ethiopia and the rest of Africa. Nimrod, "the mighty hunter before the Lord" (Genesis 10:9), was a descendent of Ham.

The Shemites, later called Semites, would become the Jews of the nation of Israel and the Arab nations that evolved from his son, Ishmael. In fact, most middle eastern people descended from Shem — including Abraham's ultimate promised Seed, mankind's Savior, Jesus Christ.

Ham — The Father of the Black Race

For centuries it has been widely accepted by biblical scholars that the black race originated from Ham, just as Herbert Lockyer in *All the Men of the Bible* states:

> The Hebrew word for Ham means "hot" and is surely prophetic of the climates that have created the blackness of the skin of the Negro, and the dark complexions of other peoples from the same stock....The Egyptian word for "Ham" is *Kem*, meaning black and warm. From Ham we have the Egyptians, Africans, Babylonians, Philistines and Canaanites.[1]

The blacks of today are descendants of Ham through his four sons:

> Ham produced four sons — Cush, Mizraim, Put and Canaan — and through his sons the tribes of Ham put down roots to form a family tree with branches that spread throughout the world. People of color, those of you with swarthy skin, those of you with brown, black and burnt faces, you are the descendants of Ham. Trace your roots, and they will lead you to Egypt, Africa and the Middle East..."[2]

Was Blackness a Curse?

The fact that Ham was the father of the black race has been used against blacks in times past. Some still believe that God cursed Ham with his black color because of his sin against his father, Noah. Some "Christians" even used our identity with Ham to justify slavery. So let's examine this idea and put it to rest.

> And Noah began to be an husbandman, and he planted a vineyard: And he drank of the wine, and was drunken; and he was uncovered within his tent.
> And Ham, the father of Canaan, saw the nakedness of his

father, and told his two brethren without. And Shem and Japheth took a garment, and laid it upon both their shoulders, and went backward, and covered the nakedness of their father; and their faces were backward, and they saw not their father's nakedness.

And Noah awoke from his wine, and knew what his younger son had done unto him. And he said, Cursed be Canaan; a servant of servants shall he be unto his brethren.

And he said, Blessed be the Lord God of Shem; and Canaan shall be his servant. God shall enlarge Japheth, and he shall dwell in the tents of Shem; and Canaan shall be his servant (Gen. 9:20-27).

A careful examination of this passage reveals that Noah's curse was not on Ham, but on Canaan, Ham's son. Perhaps this was so because Ham failed as a son to honor his father. Since God visits the sins of the fathers upon the children (Ex. 20:5), Ham may have "reaped exactly as he had sown — Ham sinned as a *son and was punished in his son!*[3]

But this certainly wasn't the perpetual curse of blackness and servitude on Ham and all his descendants that American slavemasters used to preach to their slaves to keep them in subjection.

This verse [25] has been used by many to support racial prejudice and even slavery. Noah's curse wasn't directed toward any particular race of people, but rather at the Canaanite nation (a nation that God knew would become wicked and evil).[4]

Neither did the curse on Canaan have any thing to do with skin color, because the black race originated from Ham. And the curse was just on Canaan, it wasn't on Ham or his other sons, Cush, Mizraim or Phut.

So if the curse had been black skin color, only the Canaanites would have been black. But Cush (Ethiopia), Mizraim (Egypt) and Phut (Africa) all have black inhabitants. Therefore, all the descendants of Ham are dark, not just the Canaanites.

The Curse on Canaan

How was this curse fulfilled in the Canaanites? They subsequently became servants in Palestine under David's leadership, just as it was prophesied by Noah. Biblical scholar Arthur Pink says:

> "And Canaan shall be (Shem's) servant." This received its first fulfillment in the days of Joshua — "And Joshua made them...*hewers of wood and drawers of water* for the congregation" (Josh. 9:27). The following scriptures set forth its further accomplishment:
>
> And it came to pass, when Israel was strong, that they *put the Canaanites to tribute* (Judges 1:28).
>
> And all the people that were left of the Amorites, Hittites, Perizites, Hivites, and Jebusites, which were not of the children of Israel, their children that were left after them in the land, whom the children of Israel also were not able utterly to destroy, upon those did Solomon *levy a tribute of bond service* unto this day (1 Kings 9:20, 21).[5]

Matthew Henry also explains the reference to servitude in regard to Canaan's curse:

> Those who by birth were his [Canaan's] equals shall by conquest be his lords. This certainly points at the victories obtained by Israel over the Canaanites, by which they were all either put to the sword or put under tribute (Jos. 9:23; Jdg. 1:28, 30, 33, 35).[6]

So God didn't curse Ham and all his descendants with blackness and servitude, because the curse of servitude was on Canaan. And the curse was fulfilled centuries ago...**it is finished.**

Our Ancestors — The Ancient Egyptians

Almost any Bible commentary and even most secular ancient history books will tell you that the names of Ham's sons relate to the following nations: Cush — Ethiopia; Mizraim — Egypt; Phut — Libya; and Canaan — the Canaanites of Palestine. And people accept the fact that Ham's descendants (the Ethiopians and Africans) are black. But not everyone realizes the ancient Egyptians were also dark-skinned.

Two scriptures in Psalms show us that Ham's dark-skinned descendants were in Egypt. The first, Psalm 78, refers to the plagues on Egypt during the Israelites' exodus:

22

He made a way to his anger; he spared not their souls from death, but gave their life over to the pestilence; And smote all their firstborn in Egypt; the chief of their strength in the tabernacles of Ham (vv. 50-51).

Here we see that *Egypt* is used interchangeably with *Ham*. In Psalm 105 we read the same thing:

Israel also came into Egypt; and Jacob sojourned in the land of Ham (v. 23).

So again, Egypt and Ham refer to the same country.

Racially Mixed

The inhabitants of Egypt today are racially mixed, but the original Egyptians were the same blacks that live in Africa and America today, as historian Basil Davidson points out:

It now seems perfectly clear that the vast majority of pre-dynastic Egyptians were of *continental African stock.*[7]

Egypt's location on the Mediterranean Sea near the countries of the Middle East and across the sea from Southern Europe made it easily accessible from many other nations. Therefore, Davidson states that the early populations of Egypt "undoubtedly included the descendants of incoming migrants from the Near East."[8]

Egyptians developed different physical characteristics from their African brothers because of intermarrying with the Assyrians, Persians, and others who migrated there or conquered them at different times in their history. But again, the original Egyptians were of the same black stock as those in other parts of Africa and American today.

Well-known black scholars W.E.B. Du Bois, Carter G. Woodson, and William Leo Hansberry write that the ancient Egyptians "were a mixed race which presented the same physical types and color ranges as American blacks — a people, in short, who would have been forced in the forties to sit on the back seats of the buses in Mississippi."[9]

So when the Bible speaks of black people, it doesn't use the terms "colored people," or "Negroes." It speaks of Ethiopians and Egyptians who are the historical ancestors of present-day blacks.

In the next chapter we will discover what happened to these ancient nations in the pages of the Old Testament Scriptures.

FOUR

Ancient Powers — Egypt and Ethiopia

Son of man, speak unto Pharaoh king of Egypt, and to his multitude; Whom art thou like in thy greatness? (Ez. 31:2).

The Egyptians were a great people who at one time ruled the world. They were at the top, but because of idol worship, they were taken down.

Ancient Egypt

Egypt's written history began around 3100 B.C. when tradition says King Menes united Upper and Lower Egypt setting the stage for the next three thousand years during which different dynasties of kings, or pharaohs, ruled over Egypt. The many pharaohs of Egypt were often worshipped as gods. They kept opulent courts and ensured massive irrigation projects. Pyramids were built as monuments and tombs. Temples to gods were constructed. And art, sculpture, and learning flourished.

Peace reigned for many centuries until the Egyptians learned the ways of war to expand their empire. The empire was at its peak during what is called the New Kingdom (1570 B.C. to 1342 B.C.). It was rich both culturally and commercially with slaves until their conquering by Alexander's generals who would rule there for three hundred years, with Cleopatra being the most famous of these Macedonian rulers. Then Egypt fell again, this time, to Rome in 30 B.C., and has never since been the glittering world power it once was.

Egypt was the world's center of culture and power for millennia. But it didn't last forever. Why?

25

Chancellor Williams addresses this question in his book, *The Destruction of the Black Civilization,* as he reviews the facts that 1) blacks were once the leading civilization on earth (Egypt) and 2) blacks were trailblazers in sciences, medicine, architecture, writing, etc. He continues:

The big unanswered question then, was *what had happened?* How was this highly advanced Black Civilization so completely destroyed that its people, in our times and for some centuries past, have found themselves not only behind the other peoples of the world, but as well, the color of their skin a sign of inferiority, bad luck, and the badge of the slave whether bond or free?[1]

How and why did this prosperous black civilization sink? What caused this great kingdom's fall?

Chancellor Williams does provide a historical depiction of the black nation's fall in his book. But the only infallible and absolute answer is found in the Bible — the Word of God.

According to the Bible, the reason for the Egyptian's fall was **idol worship**.

The Idols of Egypt

Since the original Egyptians were sons of Ham and grandsons of Noah, they knew about the one true God. The Egyptians were "originally monotheistic but gradually lapsed into the basest idolatry."[2] They fell into idol worship.

The first commandment of God says, "Thou shalt have no other gods before me" (Ex. 20:3). And the Egyptians worshiped false gods.

Ancient Egypt broke the first commandment of God which says, "Thou shalt have no other gods before me" (Ex. 20:3) and were famous for their many gods. Even today, school children studying Egyptian history learn about the Egyptian gods Osiris, Isis and Ra. Besides these and many others, each town had a town-god and crafts had their own gods as well.

Some Egyptian gods were pictured as humans, others as animals. Horus appeared as a hawk; Hathor was a cow. Embalmed animals have even been found in special cemeteries. The numerous statues and even the sphinx represented gods.

26

We all know that God sent plagues upon Egypt when Pharaoh refused to set the Israelites free (Ex. 8). Warren Wiersbe agrees with many other scholars when he states, "The plagues were God's declaration of war against the false gods of Egypt."[3]

Willmington's Guide to the Bible lists the gods the that plagues were directed against:

(1) The first plague of bloody waters was directed against Osiris, the god of the Nile.

(2) The second plague of frogs was against the frog goddess Hekt.

(3) The third plague of lice was against Seb, the earth god.

(4) The fourth plague of beetles (or flies) was against Hatkok, the wife of Osiris.

(5) The fifth plague of cattle disease was against Apis, the sacred bull god.

(6) The sixth plague, boils, was against Typhon.

(7) The seventh plague, hail and fire, was against Shu, the god of the atmosphere.

(8) The eighth plague, locusts, was against Serapia, the god who protected Egypt against locusts.

(9) The ninth plague, darkness, was against Ra, the sun god.

(10) The tenth plague, the death of the firstborn, was an attack on *all* gods.[4]

So all ten of these infamous plagues marked the beginning of the fall of Egypt.

Prophecy Against Egypt

The Exodus plagues happened around 1400 B.C. Then around 710 B.C., God told the prophet Isaiah to prophesy against Egypt. He used prophets like Isaiah to tell people about future events and to make His will known to man. God saw the idolatry of Egypt, and He was ready to do something about it.

Now let's look at Isaiah 19 to see God's prophecy against Egypt:

The burden of Egypt. Behold, the Lord rideth upon a swift cloud, and shall come into Egypt: and the idols of Egypt shall be moved at his presence, and the heart of Egypt shall melt in the midst of it (Is. 19:1).

In this verse God said He would destroy the idol gods, and ancient Egypt would fall.

> And I will set the Egyptians against the Egyptians: and they shall fight every one against his brother, and every one against his neighbour; city against city, and kingdom against kingdom (v. 2).

The prophecy goes on to reveal how the Egyptians would destroy themselves by quarreling among themselves. As Jesus said, "If a kingdom be divided against itself, that kingdom cannot stand" (Mark 3:24).

> Whenever we see in a nation social dissension setting in, unity and co-operation no longer possible, it is sign that a new force is at work...that "God has awoke to judgment."[5]

So part of God's judgment against Egypt would consist of a spirit of disunity and infighting. And because Egypt would lose its ability to make good judgments, verse 3 says the people would turn to sorcery and wizards for advice and counsel.

> And the spirit of Egypt shall fail in midst thereof; and I shall destroy the counsel thereof: and they shall seek to the idols, and to the charmers, and to them that have familiar spirits, and to the wizards (v. 3).

Now in verse 4 we find the first mention of slavery concerning Egypt. It indicates Egypt would be given over to another to be ruled over mercilessly. God is a jealous God (Deut. 5:9), and He will not be usurped by false gods.

> And the Egyptians will I give over into the hand of a cruel lord; and a fierce king shall rule over them, saith the Lord, the Lord of hosts (v. 4).

After Isaiah's prophecy was given, Egypt was enslaved by the Assyrians for forty years. Then God allowed them return to Egypt. Joyce Andrews in *Bible Legacy of the Black Race* notes:

This first scattering of the Egyptians, over a period of forty years, more or less, was obviously intended to dissolve the culture and the lifestyle of the Egyptians, making it impossible for them to reestablish Egyptian society as it formerly was.[6]

But Egypt was later conquered again by nearby nations, then the Greeks and Romans. This series of events brought about Egypt's ultimate fall.

And the waters shall fail from the sea, and the river shall be wasted and dried up. And they shall turn the rivers far away; and the brooks of defence shall be emptied and dried up: the reeds and flags shall whither. The paper reeds by the brooks, by the mouth of the brooks, and every thing sown by the brooks, shall wither, be driven away, and be no more (vv. 5-7).

Verses 5 through 7 indicated how Egypt's land would be cursed by God with drought. This prophecy has plagued Egypt and Africa for centuries, and it has yet to be restored. Whenever something happens to land, a larger force is at work. Only God can dry up land. So His spiritual force is at work in this drought.

The fishers also shall mourn, and all they that cast angle into the brooks shall lament, and they that spread nets upon the waters shall languish. Moreover they that work in fine flax, and they that weave networks, shall be confounded. And they shall be broken in the purposes thereof, all that make sluices and ponds for fish (vv. 8-10).

Egypt was also known for its fishing and flax industries. The linens of Egypt were renowned and its garments were glamorous. But the prophecy in verses 8-10 revealed it would all come to an end — because of idolatry.

Surely the princes of Zoan are fools, the counsel of the wise counsellors of Pharaoh is become brutish (v. 11a).

Now verse 11 is very interesting because it shows how the Egyptians ended up in the wilderness on the plains and in the jungles of Africa. The princes of Zoan represented the counsellors of Egypt who would no longer have the ability to advise Pharaoh. Verse 11 says they would become brutish (animal-like) or stupid. The Lord made them brutish just as he made Nebuchadnezzar animal-like to show him that he was nothing compared to God:

They shall drive thee [Nebuchadnezzar] from men, and thy dwelling shall be with the beasts of the field, and they shall make thee to eat grass as oxen, and they shall wet thee with the dew of heaven...till thou know that the most High ruleth in the kingdom of men (Dan. 4:25).

Just as Nebuchadnezzar was made animal-like and driven into the fields, so the Egyptians were made brutish and driven into the bush land (see Ezek. 29:5).

How say ye unto Pharaoh, I am the son of the wise, the son of the ancient kings (v.11b).

After Egypt's fall, people would never believe that the people living in the bush were ever grand and majestic. Their fall would be so great, and they would be so brutish and unrefined, this second half of verse 11 indicates, that no one would believe they used to be kings.

Where are they? Where are thy wise men? And let them tell thee now, and let them know what the Lord of hosts hath purposed upon Egypt. The princes of Zoan are become fools, the princes of Noph are deceived; they have also seduced Egypt, even they that are the stay of the tribes thereof (vv. 12-13).

Egypt's wise men were the stay, the foundation, of the nation. Everybody depended upon them for leadership. But God would destroy their leadership and the people's dependency on them.

The Lord hath mingled a perverse spirit in the midst thereof: and they have caused Egypt to err in every work thereof, as a

30

drunken man staggereth in his vomit (v. 14).

So in the end, instead of being successful and leading the nations, Egypt would stagger and become perverse. The sophistication and refinement the kingdom had know for thousands of years would disappear.

Neither shall there be any work for Egypt, which the head or tail, branch or rush, may do (v. 15).

Verse 15 shows that Egypt's prosperity would of course fail in their fall. No one would find any way to make a living or succeed at any work.

In that day shall Egypt be like unto women: and it shall be afraid and fear because of the shaking of the hand of the Lord of hosts, which he shaketh over it (v. 16).

The Egyptian army was the greatest on earth at one time because they weren't afraid of death. Life after death was crucial to them, and they looked forward to it. So they had a kamikaze mentality when it came to death. But verse 16 reveals how God made them afraid in order to conquer them.

And the land of Judah shall be a terror unto Egypt, every one that maketh mention thereof shall be afraid in himself, because of the counsel of the Lord of hosts, which he hath determined against it (v. 17).

The great and impervious Egypt would become afraid of other lands and other governments.

Into the Bush

God sent Isaiah and other prophets to warn the Egyptians about their idolatry. He desired their repentance and return to Him, but they didn't do it. They stayed in their sin, so God acted.

And I will leave thee *thrown into the wilderness*, thee and all the fish of thy rivers: thou shalt fall upon the open fields; thou shalt not be brought together, nor gathered: I have given thee for meat to the beasts of the field and to the fowls of the heaven (Ezek. 29:5).

Here again is a very revealing verse that shows how the Egyptians ended up in the wilderness on the plains and in the jungles of Africa. God deposed the Egyptians from their great cities and grandeur. Then He "threw" them into the wilderness and left them there, to live in the bush land. And that's where the European slave traders found them, scattered in different tribes in different parts of Africa.

I will scatter the Egyptians among the nations, and will disperse them through the countries (v. 12b).

God foresaw that the blacks would be taken to countries all around the world, but not by their own choice. They would be taken as slaves, and now they are all over the world.

Egypt and Ethiopia — Sister Nations

Prophecies like those that fell upon Egypt also came upon Ethiopia because they were sister nations. Remember that Ham's son Mizraim settled Egypt and his son Cush settled Ethiopia. Historian Chancellor Williams calls Egypt, "Ethiopia's Oldest Daughter."[7] He goes on to say:

The ancient Ethiopian Empire [is] the "Heartland of the Race" — the motherland with a civilization that, despite the Asian invasions, still included all Upper Egypt in 3100 B.C., and extended southward over the Sudan across Abyssinia.[8]

Social historian and writer Lerone Bennett adds:

There was long and intimate contact between the dark-skinned Egyptians and the dark-skinned Ethiopians. For fifty centuries or more they fought, traded and intermarried.[9]

So we can see that Egypt and Ethiopia are linked together in history. And they are also linked prophetically in the Bible. The fall of both was prophesied by Isaiah around 713 B.C.:

At that same time spake the Lord by Isaiah the son of Amoz, saying, Go and loose the sackcloth from off thy loins, and put off thy shoe from thy foot. And he did so, walking naked and barefoot.

And the Lord said, Like as my servant Isaiah hath walked naked and barefoot three years for a sign and wonder upon Egypt and upon Ethiopia; So shall the king of Assyria lead away the Egyptians prisoners, and the Ethiopians captives (20:2-4a).

Another example of this linkage is found in Ezekiel 30:

And the sword shall come upon Egypt, and great pain shall be in Ethiopia, when the slain shall fall in Egypt, and they shall take away her multitude, and her foundations shall be broken down (v. 4).

Chastisement for Idolatry

The prophecies concerning Egypt and Ethiopia point to dismal events — suffering, enslavement and the loss of their homelands. Captivity would await the Egyptians and Ethiopians along with their descendants.

All of these things came upon the Egyptians and Ethiopians because of idolatry. They chose to worship man-made idols instead of the true and living God.

Now I must tell you, though I was proud when I learned the Egyptians were my ancestors, and that my heritage stemmed from a regal, dignified people, I also felt tremendous sorrow for myself and for my people when I realized we were punished by God and fell. I looked for justification from God. Was it just of Him to punish my ancestral idol worshippers with slavery, captivity, and servitude? It also made me wonder if we were the only people who committed the crime of idolation and were judged with enslavement.

Then I found that He did the same thing to Israel when Israel went after false gods. So in the next chapter we will look back in history to see how God enslaved Israel because of idol worship, not just once, but many times.

FIVE

The Biblical Account of Slavery

Righteousness exalts a nation, but sin is a reproach to *any* people (Prov. 14:34).

S in always evokes a reaction from God. So when a people substitute an idol for the true and living God, He reacts. In fact, God has a routine reaction to any nation who turns to idol worship and gross sinfulness: He puts that nation under subjection to another until they cry out to Him and desire to return to Him.

This truth should eradicate the idea that the blacks were the only ones who were judged. Israel itself was subjected to the chastisement of slavery.

Israel Enslaved Four Hundred Years

In Genesis 15, the Lord predicted that Israel would be enslaved four hundred years.

And he said unto Abram, Know of a surety that thy seed shall be a stranger in a land that is not theirs, and shall serve them; and they shall afflict them four hundred years (v. 13).

The prophecy came to pass and Israel was enslaved under the Egyptians just over four hundred years (Ex. 12:40). So the Egyptians were the first slave masters, used by God to chastise Israel.

The Israelites went to Egypt because of a famine in their own land. God used Joseph to prepare the way for them. But once there, the people were seduced by, and worshipped, Egypt's gods. How do we know this? After Moses led them out of Egypt, as soon as the going got tough, they fashioned a golden calf that represented an Egyptian god and worshipped it. They reverted to their old Egyptian ways.

God is a just God who doesn't punish without cause. The real crime was revealed in the wilderness as Israel's true character was revealed. God foresaw that they would worship the idol gods of Egypt, so He prophesied His reaction — their enslavement.

The Pattern: Idolatry, Bondage, Repentance, Deliverance

After the Israelites left Egypt to enter their Promised Land, they disobeyed God and went after the false gods of the lands they were conquering. And every time Israel turned from God to worship idols, God enslaved them. Then they cried out to God, and he sent them a deliverer. The theme in the Book of Judges is defeat and deliverance:

Judges records the activities of twelve men and one woman designated as judges and raised up by God to deliver Israel in the time of sin, degradation, and disunity after Joshua's death. The four-fold cycle so common in Israel's history (rebellion, retribution, repentance, and restoration) occurs repeatedly. Joshua is a book of victory; Judges is a book of defeat.[1]

The Israelites experienced a brief season of success in the day of Joshua, but after his death, they turned to the Gentile's idols.

And the children of Israel did evil in the sight of the Lord, and forgat the Lord their God, and served Baalim and the groves. Therefore the anger of the Lord was hot against Israel, and he sold them into the hand of Chushan-rishathaim king of Mesopotamia: and the children of Israel served Chushan-rishathaim eight years. And when the children of Israel cried unto the Lord, the Lord raised up a deliverer to the children of Israel, who delivered them, even Othniel the son of Kenaz, Caleb's younger brother (Judg. 3:7-9).

The people turned from God to idols; God enslaved them; they cried out to Him; then He sent a deliverer for them. This pattern is well-established in God's Word. It happened over and over.

> And the children of Israel did evil again in the sight of the Lord:
> and the Lord strengthened Eglon the king of Moab against
> Israel, because they had done evil in the sight of the Lord. And
> he gathered unto him the children of Ammon and Amalek, and
> went and smote Israel, and possessed the city of palm trees. So
> the children of Israel served Eglon the king of Moab eighteen
> years. But when the children of Israel cried unto the Lord, the
> Lord raised them up a deliverer, Ehud the son of Gera, a
> Benjamite, a man left handed (Judg. 3:12-15).

The point to be made is that God raised up a nation to enslave His
people Israel: "The Lord strengthened Eglon the king of Moab against
Israel, because they had done evil in the sight of the Lord." God
strengthened the oppressor in order to chastise the Israelites.

So even God's chosen people demonstrated recidivism, a constant
falling away. They went through a biblically recorded pattern first, of
sinning. Then they were conquered or enslaved. Then they repented and
cried out to the Lord. Then the Lord would raise up a deliverer to free
them. Then the cycle would begin again.

> And the children of Israel did evil in the sight of the Lord: and
> the Lord delivered them into the hand of the Midians seven
> years (Judg. 6:1).

In this passage of Judges 6 when Israel sinned, God raised up the
Midianites to chastise the nation. Then when the people finally cried out,
God sent Gideon to deliver them.

Israel's testimony provides historical proof that the sin of idolatry
infuriates God to the point of harsh judgment. And slavery seems to be
the ultimate punishment for this sin. But was it over yet? No.

> And the children of Israel did evil again in the sight of the Lord;
> and the Lord delivered them into the hand of the Philistines forty
> years (Judg. 13:1).

Anyone who reads through the Book of Judges will feel as if they're on a real roller coaster ride. The Israelites climb up to God and are set free; then they race back down into idolatry. And every time they do it, God sends them into some form of bondage. Then they climb back up to the top when in response to their repentance, God sends a deliverer.

> If ye forsake the Lord, and serve strange gods, then he will turn and do you hurt, and consume you, after that he hath done you good (Josh. 24:20).

It is universally true that nations who forget God will be chastised and that God has used slavery in the past to bring about chastisement that leads to righteousness. Slavery was not unique to the Israelites, or to the black people. God is an awesome God, and He will do anything He wants to do, even if it hurts those He needs to do it to.

No nation can go against a sovereign, mighty God and not expect a reaction. Greece went the same route because of idol worship. Rome fell because of decadence and their lack of reverence for God. Both exalted men as idols, and neither has ever risen from out of their demise. They are proverbs, relics of the past.

The Chosen Instrument

Egypt was God's chosen instrument used to enslave Israel four hundred years. Then when Egypt rejected the prophets' warnings against their own idolatry, its role changed and they were given over "into the hand of a cruel lord" (19:4). They became the enslaved rather than the slave master.

In time God would choose another instrument to serve as the scattered Egyptian's slave master. As I sat that wonderful day in that airplane crying, I was set free. Because it was then that I realized who sent the ships across that vast, dangerous ocean pictured in the airline magazine — and why they were sent.

SIX

Who Sent the Ships?

In that day shall messengers go forth from me in ships....
(Ez. 30:9).

If you ever want to know the mindset of a black man, go to a black barber shop. When you do you will hear discussions about politics, religion, sports — and, of course, racial problems.

One day after God healed me on the airplane, I walked into one of the main black barber shops in Orlando, Florida. The men in there were having a heated discussion about the injustices of the American system. The brothers were venting and protesting about how the white man's system was totally against black progress.

This particular day the brothers were vehemently enumerating the many injustices each had encountered during their lifetimes. One man was going on about the lack of jobs, the lack of recreational parks, the injustices of the school system, and the inequality of whites and blacks in general.

"Look at our neighborhood," he said. "There are no parks in the neighborhood for our kids to play in like in the white neighborhoods. There are no jobs for our black men. Why should they work at McDonald's or Burger King for minimum wage when they can sell dope on the corner and make more in one day than they can in a month at a fast food place?"

He got louder and louder, feeling justified in his rage. It was like they were having church and he was the preacher with all the other brothers saying, "Amen."

Earlier in my life I would have joined in with them and stolen the man's pulpit. But there is something about the truth. When you know it, it will make you free — and God had made me free on the airplane that day.

I questioned whether I should sit and listen to their heated dismay about the system or if I should even enter the discussion. Then I heard this man say, "We were over in Africa, minding our own business, when all of a sudden the white man decided to enslave us out of his greed and hatred for blacks. They brought us over here in the ships...."

Who's Really To Blame?

That was all I could take. So I stood up and said, "Brothers, we blame the white man for everything." They knew I was a preacher, so they listened to me respectfully. "But our real problem is with God, not with the white man." That got their attention. All eyes were on me, as they waited to hear how I would explain this outrageous statement.

"We were in Egypt," I continued, "in power for three thousand years. We are indeed the descendants of Egyptians. We were scientists and inventors, educators and writers."

Well, they liked that. Because whenever you talk about blacks being descendants of the great civilization of ancient Egypt, you get our attention because we have been put down so much and so long. Whenever we hear anything that gives us any credibility or validation, we perk up.

Then I added, "But that also means we were the first slave masters. We enslaved Israel for four hundred years." Now they were surprised.

"We were on top, but now we're not because we picked a fight with God." Now they were very surprised. Then I noticed a Bible on the counter, so I picked it up. Even with the Islamic influence in the black community, most blacks still fear and respect the Bible. I started reading some of the verses in Isaiah 19 that spoke about God's judgment of Egypt because of its idolatry, witchcraft, and sorcery. I talked about the idols we worshipped in Africa. Then I showed them the first mention of slavery:

> And the Egyptians will I give over into the hand of a cruel lord; and a fierce king shall rule over them, saith the Lord, the Lord of hosts (v. 4).

They cried in disbelief, "You mean to say God permitted that to happen?"

So I responded, "Yes, because He did it before with Israel and any other nation who turned from Him."

But the real bomb dropped when I got to the ships. I flipped to Ezekiel 30 and read:

> In that day shall messengers go forth from me in ships to make the careless Ethiopians afraid, and great pain shall come upon them, as in the day of Egypt: for, lo, it cometh (v. 9).

"The Lord sent the ships to pick us up," I said quietly, waiting for everything to sink in. "He raised up the white man to bring the ships to pick us up and enslave us." Now there was absolute silence in that barber shop.

One of the men there was in ministry and wanted to see where I read from. When I showed him, he confirmed it to everyone. "It's in there," he said.

So I decided to continue in Ezekiel. Though they were shocked, the missing pieces of the puzzle had to be added.

The Vexed Heart of the White Man

"I now want to tell you why the white man can't stand us," I announced. Then I read:

> I will also vex the hearts of many people, when I shall bring thy destruction among the nations, into the countries which thou has not known (Ez. 32:9).

"God vexed the white man's heart against us — the black race," I said somberly. His heart is irritated at us." Well that was it. That was the knock-out punch. You could hear the parking meters ticking outdoors.

Absolute Truth

So when I was finished, I sat down. Everyone was silent. Then the young man sitting next to me said quietly, "I knew something was wrong." He said he reasoned that we must have done something wrong to be at the bottom of the totem pole, economically stripped as we are.

But he had never heard the truth before.

Most men in black barber shops can get rather philosophical. I call them pseudo-Aristotles, -Platos and -Euripides. They espouse a perspective of relative truth in the philosophies of radical revolutionaries. I came in with an absolute. And my absolute truth brought absolute silence. But I felt as if I could hear the conversations taking place inside of them. That's why I believe God did some healing in that barber shop that day.

Prophecies Fulfilled

It was proven to me that many prophecies were fulfilled through the sending of the slave ships. Ezekiel 30:9 shows that God sent the ships. It's worth quoting again:

> In that day shall messengers go forth from me in ships to make
> the careless Ethiopians afraid, and great pain shall come upon
> them, as in the day of Egypt: for, lo, it cometh.

Other prophecies against idolatry were also fulfilled through the enslavement of the blacks. Though spoken specifically against Israel, God spoke judgment in Deuteronomy 28 upon any who would disobey His commandments to "go after other gods to serve them" (v. 14).

> But it shall come to pass, if thou wilt not hearken unto the voice
> of the Lord thy God, to observe to do all his commandments and
> his statutes which I command thee this day; that all these curses
> shall come upon thee, and overtake thee (v. 15).

We cringe when we hear about curses. That word *curse* shakes people up, and it ought to.

God said Israel would be cursed everywhere they went (v. 16). And that He would send pestilence and disease (vv. 21-22). The heavens would be like brass (v. 23). They would "be removed into all the kingdoms of the earth" (v. 25). They would "beget sons and daughters, but thou shalt not enjoy them; for they shall go into captivity (v. 41).

Look at Africa today. Missionaries and medical personnel are constantly serving our people there due to pestilence and disease. The heavens are like brass in many areas because of severe drought. We as a people have been scattered over the whole earth. The slaves' families

42

were separated, and their children were sold. And these curses followed the black man into those ships.

Betrayal

The Portuguese, Dutch, French, Swedes, Danes, Prussians, Arabs and Spaniards could never have succeeded in capturing the Africans if the Africans had been unified. But they weren't. Historian Jeffrey Stewart tells us:

> It is a myth that most Africans who became slaves in America were captured by Europeans in slave raids. Most of the Africans who became slaves were sold into slavery by other Africans."[1]

African kings and tribal chiefs sold their prisoners of war from other tribes to the slave traders. This gave them the resources necessary to maintain the prisoners, and they profited as well.[2] Some traded slaves for firearms, which only led to more tribal wars and more opportunities for slave traders.

I also showed them in the barber shop that day how this disunity was part of our curse — because of idolatry:

> And I will set the Egyptians against the Egyptians: and they shall fight every one against his brother, and every one against his neighbor; city against city, and kingdom against kingdom (Is. 19:2).

The Slave Ships

> And the Egyptians will I give over into the hand of a cruel lord (Is. 19:4a).

Slavery was so cruel that many blacks died on the way to the ship. The paths were so bloodied and littered with bodies, they had to cut new trails.[3]

Those who made it to the ships, were stacked like sardines. Rev. John Newton (1725-1807), the famous slave trader who later converted to Christ and wrote the great spiritual anthem "Amazing Grace," wrote:
Their lodging rooms below the deck...are sometimes more than

five feet high and sometimes less; and this height is divided toward the middle for the slaves lie in two rows, one above the other, on each side of the ship, close to each other like books upon a shelf. I have known them so close that the shelf would not easily contain one more.

The poor creatures, thus cramped, and likewise in irons for the most part which makes it difficult for them to turn or move or attempt to rise or to lie down without hurting themselves or each other. Every morning, perhaps, more instances than one are found of the living and the dead fastened together.[4]

Slaves would have to lay on hard wood for six to ten weeks. Often the skin on their elbows or knees became worn to the bone, especially when the weather was rough.

The sharks would follow the ships from the coast of Africa all the way to the United States or other destinations because of the regular meals. It was common practice to throw overboard anyone with symptoms of smallpox. Slaves were also thrown into the sea to reduce the weight of the ship. And many jumped overboard to end their misery.[5]

The greatest threat to the life of a slave was disease, which spread quickly in the tight quarters.[6] These quarters were described by a British ship's surgeon as "so covered with the blood and mucus which had proceeded from them in consequence of the flux [dysentery], that it resembled a slaughter-house."[7]

What a description of the following verse:

The Lord shall smite thee with a consumption, and with a fever, and with an inflammation (Deut. 28:22).

It was the Portuguese who started the shipping slave trade. In the 1400s, Portuguese sailors began making contact with African tribes. By 1460, "seven or eight hundred slaves were being carried to Portugal annually."[8]

The Emancipation Proclamation issued by President Lincoln some four hundred years later in 1863 gave freedom to those held as slaves in America. But the slave trade did last about four hundred years. So did Israel's enslavement in Egypt. If you do the crime, you do the time. Around 12 to 13 million blacks were taken from Africa as slaves during that time period.[9] They were scattered all over Brazil, England, Spain, North America, and South America.

> And I will scatter the Egyptians among the nations, and will disperse them though the countries (Ez. 30:23).

From the ships to the plantations, the white man raped the black man's wife. "White men were frequent visitors to the slave quarters. And the offspring of such liaisons were usually held in the same low regard as their mothers."[10] The many shades of blacks there are now mostly due to these violations.

> Thou shall betroth to a wife, and another man shall lie with her (Deut. 28:30).

God is harsh with people who bow to idolatry, and slavery is a harsh chastisement.

> Therefore shalt thou serve thine enemies, which the Lord shall send against thee, in hunger, and in thirst, and in nakedness, and in want of all things: and he shall put a yoke of iron upon thy neck, until he have destroyed thee (Deut. 28:48).

Because He Loved Us

A black television minister once said he was glad the ships came. So am I. They came because God loved us too much to leave us in idolatry.

When I look at the tribal warfare that is going on in Africa and the multiplicity of problems there — drought, dissension and political wars — I'm glad that the ships came. God used drastic means to bring us out of a life of idol worship, darkness and ignorance, but He did bring us out into the knowledge of the one true God.

Plus, the black slaves in America eventually gained their freedom. This historic struggle for liberation set a precedent for the whole world. God sent deliverers such as Abraham Lincoln and Martin Luther King to release the people — both white and black — from the horrid reality of the curses on them. Freedom and deliverance for blacks everywhere began in the United States. The struggle for liberation has now traveled to other parts of the world, such as South Africa, like ripples on a pond.

NO APOLOGY NECESSARY, JUST RESPECT

Though the United States wasn't the original instigator of slavery, it became a model for deliverance from it. Black people don't want to admit this, but somebody needs to say it. Black people still believe this is a racist society, and it is in a sense. But America is where God's deliverance began.

It is a paradox, yes. I'm sorry we had to be enslaved, but I'm certainly glad the ships came.

A Loving God Hates Sin

It is hard to believe that a loving God would allow such evil to happen to the black people. It shows us how intemperate God can get when it comes to the sin of idol worship. We know these things happened, and that they're still happening because men need to turn to the truth. If God is for you, who can be against you? (Rom. 8:31). But if He's against you, the prophecy will continue.

Because of the presence of sin on earth, life isn't fair, and it won't be until sin is removed. So don't expect things to be fair.

The fact that God punished us so severely for idolatry by raising up so terrible a slave master lets us know how serious God is about sin. The wages of sin is death (Rom. 6:23). Not just sickness, but death. Not just poverty, death. Not just suffering, death. There's nothing worse than death. So, in order to rescue us from it, God sometimes uses the executioner to carry out punishment.

This is the other side of God — the side that punishes sin to rescue the sinner from death. He does all this to curb our desire to go after another God. God is a jealous God. He doesn't want us to have any other gods but Him.

Think about it. God allowed His only begotten Son to experience death through the most gruesome way to die — on the cross. Jesus suffered for hours, to take on the sin of mankind, and none of us can imagine what that was like.

So if God was willing to give up His only Son because of sin, you know He is willing to destroy anybody else who plays with it, especially the sin of idolatry.

For whom the Lord loveth he chasteneth, and scourgeth every son whom he receiveth (Heb. 12:6).

46

God told me to, "Tell the people that I did it. I did it because I loved them," because those whom He loves, He chastises. And He won't back down from the reality of what He did.

God is a God of justice and a God of love. We provoked Him to the drastic measure of grinding idolatry out of us, so now we can sing:

"Father, I stretch my hand to thee and no other help I know."

Now we don't have to be involved in idol worship any more. We don't have to serve any other god but the true and living God through His Son Jesus Christ.

I don't apologize for God. I believe He told me not to. He is God, Who does what He wants to fulfill His will. And I believe He wants everybody to know that He sent the ships.

But the prophecies didn't end with the ships. They continued to follow black people today.

SEVEN

Prophecy Continued: The Black Man Today

Part I

God warned the Egyptians through His prophets to abandon their idolatry. But, as Joyce Andrews says:

> The warning predicting the downfall of Pharaoh and the desolation of the land of Egypt went totally unheeded by the Egyptians and consequently the prophecy came to pass and fell on the Egyptians and their descendants (black people of African descent), the consequences of which are yet prevalent among black people, even to this present day![1]

Until the black man repents of idolatry, Egypt's prophecies continue to affect him. Let's see how these same prophecies from Isaiah 19 are fulfilled in the black man today.

Black Against Black

> And I will set the Egyptians against the Egyptians: and they shall fight every one against his brother, and every one against his neighbor; city against city, and kingdom against kingdom (Is. 19:2).

Have you ever wondered why we as a people can't seem to get together? God's method has always been to divide and conquer. At the tower of Babel, He confused the language of the people, dividing them and stripping them of the power of unity.

So Isaiah's prophecy has followed Egyptian descendants through the centuries. It has been my experience that we as a people seem to have unusual dislike for each other.

I related this scripture in the barber shop that day to the problems we as black Americans have today. Asians come to America and live and work together. They create a unified front and a financial base. They work hard, help each other, and buy the corner store. The next thing you know, they are prospering. But not blacks. We're divided. We've been over here for hundreds of years, and we can't even get together on a hot dog stand.

When I was sharing that day in the barber shop, one brother interrupted to tell me how much he loves his brothers and his people. I told him that I love my brothers and I love my people also, but I also told him I knew we're more subject to getting killed by a black man than a white man. And brother, dead is dead.

I really challenged him, "Brother, if you had a gold chain around your neck and diamond rings on your fingers, I could send you into a neighborhood in Philadelphia that I know you would not come back from. Your same *loving* brothers there would destroy you for what you have."

Everyone laughed, but we all knew it was true. Black-on-black crime is a reality we couldn't shake.

I continued, "In that particular neighborhood, if you saw a dozen brothers coming toward you, would you feel an urge to go hug them, or run? In the black community the bars on our windows reflect our fear of each other. We are divided, just as it was prophesied."

Brother Against Brother

When I was a little boy growing up with my brothers, we would fight like cats and dogs. The news recently reported that a black boy killed his brother over a ham sandwich. So family infighting is not unusual among blacks today.

When we lived in the projects, our neighbors fought against us and we fought against them. When the football team visiting from another city won the game when I was in school, they would lose the fight *after* the game. We would turn over their school buses.

Today black men are destroying themselves in record numbers, dying violent and reckless deaths at the hands of each other.

According to the U.S. Department of Justice, almost 7 percent of all black male adults were in jail or in prison in 1994.[2] Among nonfatal firearm injuries from mid-1992 to mid-1993, 59 percent of the victims were black. One-quarter of all those shot were black males between the ages of 15 to 24.[3]

In the mid '80s I was riding in my car one evening in Oakland, California, listening to the radio when the news came on. The reporter said a black man and his fiancé were riding on the freeway and accidentally bumped the car of two black men. So he pulled over on the side of the road to exchange insurance information. But when he looked in his pockets, he discovered he had left his wallet at home. So he said to the two men, "Follow me home so I can give you my information." The men followed the man home, and when they got there, they pulled out a .357-magnum, raped the man's fiancé and shot her in the head, point blank. Then they shot him in the shoulder as he ran outside and fell. The one doing the shooting tried to shoot him again, but the gun jammed. So they got into their car to run the man over, but he got out of the way just in time. The man lived to later identify the two black men.

A television documentary I recently watched about black-on-black crime told of how a middle-aged black man was walking on the streets of Washington, D.C., when two blacks in their late teens attacked him. One knocked the man out cold, urinated in his face, then shot him in his buttocks.

We already learned how betrayal and disunity among Africans was responsible for many of the Africans being sold into slavery in the first place. Today disunity and betrayal still exists among the slaves' descendants.

> Many rebellions were thwarted because slaves told their masters about plots. Some betrayed their fellow slaves because it was one of the surest ways to obtain one's own freedom.[4]

Many free slaves had slaves. Most well-off blacks just before the Emancipation Proclamation was signed were slavers too. They had slaves because they sold out fellow slaves in order to get their freedom.

This has followed black people — we sell each other out. We'll go behind each others' backs and say, "I can do that job better for less." We

51

underbid each other. We tell on one another. It's still common today. So I believe we can see how Isaiah's prophecy follows the people who are outside of God.

On the job our black supervisors make a special effort to let everyone know they are the boss — especially their own black counterparts. Even in the church, the way some pastors try to control people makes it seem like they are "Reverend Pharaohs" rather than servants.

Kingdom Against Kingdom

Today in Africa one tribe contends against another. The whole world knows about the one million Tutsis killed in Rwanda in 1994 by the rival tribe, the Hutus. Now the rivalry has spread to Zaire, where the Tutsi rebels are fighting the government, and the people are suffering for it.

In August 1996 in neighboring Burundi, the Tutsi military took over the country. Some 150,000 lives have been lost since the fighting started there.

And in Liberia, which was founded in 1947 by former black American slaves who returned to Africa, warring factions have caused the deaths of over 150,000 since 1990.

The Bible is absolutely true. History as well as present-day tribal warfare reveals the disunity of blacks in Africa as well as in the United States.

Before Nelson Mandela became president of South Africa, seven million whites ruled over thirty-one million blacks and other races. Why didn't the blacks rule? There was no unity among them.

In September of 1996 gansta rapper Tupac Shakur was gunned down in a gang-style hit. Six months later gansta rapper Notorious B.I.G. was killed in the same manner. Why? The newspaper said:

Many of Shakur's supporters believed Notorious B.I.G...was behind Shakur's September 1996 death.... Now many are viewing B.I.G.'s violent death as retaliation....

Some observers say...it was a battle of the coasts — between the heavier, gang-inspired gangsta rap of Shakur and West Coast cornies of Death Row Records and the high-life, put-down style of Wallace and East Coast rappers under New York-based Bad Boy Entertainment.[5]

So the prophecy has followed the people. One rapper's "kingdom" is against another rapper's "kingdom." It's tribe against tribe all over again. Matthew Henry's commentary on Isaiah 19 says "One party shall be for a thing for no other reason than because the other is against it."[6] It makes no sense, but it's true.

Hurt by Each Other

Black peoples' attitude toward one another makes it evident that something is wrong with us. I've had many bad moments with whites, but my worst moments have come from my own people. I hate to admit this, but my greatest hurts have come from my own black people. You expect others to treat you bad, but not your own.

When my white brothers go into a black restaurant or any black business, they're treated with respect, but when I go into a black restaurant, I feel like Rodney Dangerfield — because I don't get any. There is a dislike, or a bad spirit, prevalent in many black businesses for fellow blacks. And it shouldn't be that way.

Jesus said to love your neighbor as you love yourself. But if you hate yourself, you can't love your neighbor. We need healing so we can love ourselves.

Superstition and Witchcraft

Something else is prevalent in the black community today — an attraction to superstition and spiritism.

And the spirit of Egypt shall fail in the midst thereof; and I will destroy the counsel thereof (Is. 19:3a).

Remember, God took away our wisdom just as he made Nebuchadnezzar into a wild animal. That's why we as a people are somewhat behind academically. Remember, we were scientists, inventors and academicians. So he had to make us slow mentally. We were up, but the idol worship brought us down.

And they shall seek to the idols, and to the charmers, and to them that have familiar spirits, and to the wizards (Is. 19:3b).

Soothsayers and witch doctors are prominent in the black community today, and blacks are very superstitious. When we were cleaning out the church one day, a woman church member told me, "Pastor, don't sweep dirt out of your front door. That means you are sweeping people out." Superstition. If a black cat runs across your path, you get so many years of bad luck and all of that.

Today blacks often pay to consult with spiritualists, fortunetellers and the like. We see blacks on television advertising psychic advice hot lines and spiritualist 1-900 numbers. Why? Because we are the ones who taught the world "black" magic.

When I was young, my mother fell sick. She had a nervous breakdown, and she believed her neighbor whom she didn't get along with, fixed her with voodoo and worked a hex on her. For years she believed that was the cause of her problems.

Maybe there was some truth to that. In Numbers 22-23, Balak tried to get Balaam to curse Israel. But every time he tried to curse Israel, blessing came instead.

How shall I curse, whom God hath not cursed? Or how shall I defy, whom the Lord hath not defied? (Num.23:8).

The devil can only curse through witchcraft those who have already been cursed by God. So because my mother wasn't redeemed by the blood of Jesus, anyone could have probably invoked a curse on her. Superstition opens the door to witchcraft.

I wanted my mother to be well. So when my uncle told me about a lady who boasted of having power to cure my mother and to release her from the curse, we sought her out.

This lady who was over a hundred years old was known to use incantations and all kinds of potions. She was respected in her black South Carolina island community as having special powers. It was said that her son had been murdered, but no one knew who did it. So this lady talked to a snake and sent it to go find who killed her son. The next morning the sheriff was found dead with snake bites on his throat.

Whether or not the story is factual is not important. It still demonstrates the type of thinking and superstition that dominates the black community.

The lady charged me about $75 for a package that she wrapped in cloth. I was scared to look in it. She told me not to open it, but to take it to my mother to have her tie it around her neck, and to take a bath in it to take the spell away.

So I took the thing back home to Philadelphia. But before I could give it to my mother, I got saved. And when God brought me in to the knowledge of the truth, I threw the thing away. I never gave it to my mother.

I did witness to my mother, though. She died a little while afterward, but she got saved before she died and went on to glory.

The following verses clearly explain what God thinks about witch-craft:

> There shall not be found among you any one that maketh his son or his daughter to pass through the fire, or that useth divination, or an observer of times, or an enchanter, or a witch, or a charmer, or a consulter with familiar spirits, or a wizard, or a necromancer. For all that do these things are an abomination unto the Lord (Deut. 18:10-12a).

Yet, many blacks are still attracted to these sins.

After I became a minister, a young man and a young lady asked me if I could come over to their house in Philadelphia to pray for them because they were seeing shadows in their home. They believed she was being cursed by a witch. The young lady had a big stomach as if she was pregnant, but she wasn't.

So I went over to their house with another Spirit-filled preacher. He was afraid, but I was bold. When I began to plead the blood of Jesus and rebuke the devil, the woman's stomach went down. And when we saw it, the preacher who was with me exclaimed, "Wow!" He couldn't believe it.

We took her over to a saint's home to stay for a while. But she kept complaining that she wanted to go to the hospital, so they took her the next day.

At the hospital the girl's mother told me that the mother of the ex-girlfriend of her daughter's boyfriend was working witchcraft on her daughter to get the boy back.

When I told her, "That lady is going to hell for working witchcraft," she showed me a Prince Albert tobacco can and said, "Don't worry. I got my root working, too." That's a prevalent statement in the black community.

I tried to see the young lady in her hospital room, but she had allowed a demon to lie to the doctors and nurses blaming me as the cause of her problem to keep me from helping her.

Because of the prophecy, blacks are still attracted to witchcraft. There's a street in South Philadelphia called South Street that is lined with little stores that have witchcraft paraphernalia. You can buy potions for everything from how to keep your man, to how to get rid of your enemy.

Witchcraft, voodoo, and fortune-telling were brought by the black people over here from Egypt. It is part of the prophecy against the Egyptians that we still see today.

But there's even more in the prophecies that we still see in blacks today.

EIGHT

Prophecy Continued: The Black Man Today

Part II

When we think of the origins of African Americans, we automatically think slavery. And when we consider the struggles for human rights black Americans have had to go through, we automatically think of oppression and humiliation. These were part of Isaiah's prophecy too.

Slavery and Oppression

> And the Egyptians will I give over into the hand of a cruel lord; and a fierce king shall rule over them, saith the Lord, the Lord of hosts (Is. 19:4).

This is the first mention of slavery for the Egyptians. We, their descendants, have suffered the fulfillment of that prophecy for over four hundred years. Even today, it is a constant battle for equal rights. Oppression is a byword for blacks around the world. In America we are still the underclass. In South Africa, blacks are just beginning to be recognized as human beings.

Though blacks were freed from slavery by the Emancipation Proclamation, we have new slave masters now. Today many blacks are ruled over by the cruel lords of drugs, alcohol, lust and the quest for black power. This prophecy still hangs on, following the descendants of the idol-worshipping Egyptians.

A Brutish Spirit

Surely the princes of Zoan are fools, the counsel of the wise counsellors of Pharaoh is become brutish: how say ye unto Pharaoh, I am the son of the wise, the son of ancient kings (v. 11).

This brutishness prophesied by Isaiah hangs upon the black people today. When we as blacks say that we are from kings and pharaohs, it's hard for people to believe because we've been in the jungle with a brutish, wild animal-like spirit for so long. He left us in the jungle until we lost our refinement to deprogram us. Therefore, people won't believe we are descendants of the Egyptians because most nations, especially the whites, believe we came from the bush land.

Our history was blotted out. The world didn't know our illustrious history, and neither did we until recently.

The reason that black history is so very important is because God would be unjust to have a people born animal-like and forbidden to progress like everyone else. But God is love, so it is inconceivable that God would treat a people like that. He is too loving.

I found that knowing black history is part of our healing, because we can never be healed unless we know who we are. God had to leave some of us there in the bush with a brutish spirit to let us understand the seriousness of the crime. Black jungle people still scar their faces, put dung in their hair, pull out their lips, put bones in their noses, and sharpen their teeth. All you have to do is look at the Discovery Channel and National Geographic to know that. We still have a remnant in the bush land of Africa who can't deal with the civilized world because they yet have that brutish spirit.

Refinement of Egypt Lost

Some of the dress and hair styles prevalent among blacks today don't reflect refinement — they are pseudo-Afrocentric. There is a difference between real Afrocentric dressing, that is refined, and pseudo-Afrocentric dressing that reflects the bush land.

So to reflect our history, our hair needs to be fashioned with sophistication. Some of the outlandish braiding popular today that looks like Africans in the bush depicted in the movies of the '30s and '40s — is animal-like, not refined or polished.

58

Some brothers wear their pants down showing their buttocks. I'm talking about the butt out. In Isaiah 20, this represents the shame of our curse:

So shall the king of Assyria lead away the Egyptians prisoners, and the Ethiopians captives, young and old, naked and barefoot, *even with their buttocks uncovered*, to the shame of Egypt (v. 4).

Some of our brothers don't understand the difference between brutish and refined.

On a recent airplane flight I saw a brother with a pseudo Afro-centric style and a boom box walk down the aisle. And lo and behold, while he was sitting down I actually saw his butt. He didn't even have on underwear. I was so embarrassed.

But I know that I have to be very sensitive because I don't want any black man like that to think I'm picking on him. I really felt sorry for him because I'm a black man too, yet I think of myself as somewhat polished, refined, and sophisticated.

But he had the look of one who is not healed. I was angry at the fact that he didn't know any better, but I wasn't angry at him. That's why a healing is necessary; so my brothers can understand the difference between refinement and brutishness.

When I was recently flying home from Buffalo, New York, a black man, his wife, mother-in-law, sister-in-law and four kids came aboard. They were conspicuously loud. So here again, I found it embarrassing.

If I hadn't known the truth, I would probably still have been angry. But because I knew the truth, I didn't look at them with disgust. I understood the brutish spirit upon them.

I mean, these people were extra loud, and the whites on the plane were quiet and civil, but I could read their minds. *Here comes Africa*, is what I imagined they were thinking.

The whites who were sitting next to me were very understanding. They were observing, but they knew they couldn't say anything to each other because I was sitting there. I felt like they really couldn't say too much because I was there to represent the refinement of Egypt rather than the brutish spirit of my black brother and his family.

The children were wild. And when this black woman told her sister to be quiet, she got louder, and said, "I spent $1,200 for this flight and I can get as loud as I want to." That gave me a further understanding of the perverse spirit that was prevalent in this lady.

So I finally spoke to them, not criticizing them, because the lady looked at me and smiled as though to say, "I know we're being ugly, but it's almost like we can't help it." She was almost apologizing and seemed to be a very intelligent young lady, but, she was sort of wild. I saw that clamourish, brutish spirit on her husband when his son tried to sit on the seat near the window. His father told him he couldn't sit there because he wasn't old enough.

The son didn't like that, so he kept saying, "Why? Why?" But that only provoked his father, who screamed — "Because you're eight years old! Sit down!" That's not refinement. He seemed to be an intelligent young man, but that brutish spirit was upon him.

A Perverse Spirit

The Lord hath mingled a perverse spirit in the midst thereof: and they have caused Egypt to err in every work thereof, as a drunken man staggereth in his vomit (v. 14).

When you talk about Egypt, you think of refinement. But here God prophesied that He was going to mingle a perverse spirit among the Egyptians.

The Egyptians were known for their excellence in work. The pyramids are an example of that. Because of the prophecy, however, we now "err in every work," and we have lost our edge in excellent work.

Once I had a black landscape worker come to work on my yard. When he put down the fertilizer, it got all over the sidewalk and stained it. The stains are still there. He cut the grass wrong. I tried to work with him, but nothing got better, so I had to let him go.

In Philadelphia I went to a black dentist for a temporary false tooth (a flipper). The flipper didn't fit, but he tried to make it work anyway. So I got angry, and told him "I can't believe you being an educated man, are so mediocre at your work."

On another occasion I took an expensive suit to a black cleaners, and they destroyed it. I made them pay for it.

I feel sorrow at having to write these things. But now I know the problem is not the people, it is the prophecy on us.

This perverse spirit is reflected in the way we talk. In the black vernacular, if you call something "bad," that means it's good. When a black man says, "Man, you're bad!" that means, "You're great!" And if somebody says, "Man, you're rank," that means you're good at what you do.

Back in my days *funky* meant a foul odor. But in the black community today when you say somebody is funky, it means he is so good at what he does he "stinks" with success.

> Woe unto them that call evil good, and good evil; that put darkness for light, and light for darkness; that put bitter for sweet, and sweet for bitter! (Is. 5:20).

So we are perverse. The black man even wears his baseball cap backward.

Once when I went to minister in a church in another city, a young man picked me up for dinner. He had his hat pulled to the side, so I rebuked him, "You need to straighten your hat up if you're going to be with me because you are now a Christian. You have to reflect refinement." "I'm sorry; it's a habit," he said sheepishly. "I can hardly help myself." I knew he was right because that spirit was upon him.

And today our poor white brothers are being influenced by the black brothers. That's why God told Israel, "Don't go to Egypt" (Jer. 42:19; Ezek. 30:7), because Egypt has a great influence on others.

You can put a black man in a white community and before long he will have white teenagers saying, "Wuz happ'ning, Yo!" If you put a white man in a black community he won't have black folks saying, "By George, by golly." Why? We simply have that dominant influence even on the white people.

So we need healing. Not all of the blacks in the ghetto are brutish because the healing started a long time ago. But many are still caught up into the "ghetto-nization" of the brutish experience — loud talking, frequent fights at parties, black-on-black crime, blacks killing blacks for frivolous reasons.

Unemployment

> Neither shall there be any work for Egypt, which the head or tail, branch or rush, may do (Is. 19:15)

Unemployment in the black community is another judgment against us. It has followed us even over here. The inability to find jobs is the constant complaint among blacks.

If you as a black are working anywhere, making any kind of money, you had better thank God because the curse is that you won't find employment.

The following prophecy about fear and terror is best understood with one from Ezekiel, but let's read Isaiah first:

> In that day shall Egypt be like unto women: and it shall be afraid and fear because of the shaking of the hand of the Lord of hosts, which he shaketh over it. And the land of Judah shall be a terror unto Egypt, every one that maketh mention thereof shall be afraid in himself, because of the counsel of the Lord of hosts, which he hath determined against it (vv. 16-17).

> Yea I will make many people amaze at thee, and their kings shall be horribly afraid for thee, when I shall brandish my sword before them; and they shall tremble at every moment, every man for his own life, in the day of thy fall (Ezek. 32:10).

These prophecies indicated that people are going to be afraid of us, and that we are going to be afraid of them. That's why the black man is afraid of the police and the police are afraid of him. The white people are afraid of the black man because of his precipitous lifestyle. And the black man is afraid of the white man because of the authority he holds over him.

Results of Prophecies

It is clear that the prophecies against Egypt follow blacks today. In fact, the characteristics of blacks today were formed by these prophecies. You can see that in black-on-black crime and betrayal, the unyielding belief in witchcraft and superstition, the brutish spirit and lack of refinement, the prevalent unemployment, the fear blacks have toward authority, and the fear they engender in others.

Men love darkness instead of light because their deeds are evil (John 3:19). We have a tendency as a people to turn to the witch doctors, soothsayers and others who are the present-day "wise men of Egypt" — men such as Louis Farrakhan of the Nation of Islam. But God is against these counselors. He is a jealous God (Deut. 5:9).

Black people seeking those who can shed light on their problems are often attracted to men who are like the flickering lights of candles. Each of these modern "wise men of Egypt" represent candles or flickering lights of hope. However, a man's light is feeble when compared to the sun. Farrakhan's light will soon be out, but the Son of God will shine forever.

In the next chapter let's see why Farrakhan's flickering candle attracts so many black people, and compare his light — to the Son of God.

NINE

Christianity's Answer to Farrakhan

———————

If black people expect anybody to apologize to them, then it simply means they haven't accepted the truth that God is right about our history, that He is right about our idolatry. He was right to do what He did to bring about the recompense of judgment.

However, and in this chapter we will get to the core of the matter, if we as blacks accept our responsibility and allow God to heal us, the next step is to change our thinking patterns. We need to learn some new patterns and forget some old ones.

Let Go of the Anger and Rage

The spiritual emancipation proclamation has been signed, sealed and delivered to us through Jesus. So the black man needs to stop talking about the past; he needs to quit dwelling on the past.

> This one thing I do, forgetting those things which are behind, and reaching forth unto those things which are before, I press toward the mark for the prize of the high calling of God in Christ Jesus (Phil. 3:13:14).

You can't do anything about the past, but you can do something about your present that will impregnate your life to give birth to a healthy future.

We must let go of the venom and the resentment. They will eat us up on the inside to make us slaves of our own venom and anger.

Many blacks are enslaved by rage and resentment, and Louis Farrakhan of the Nation of Islam represents that anger and rage. This is why many blacks are attracted to him, because they don't know the truth. The Bible tells us not to follow an angry man.

> Make no friendship with an angry man; and with a furious man thou shalt not go: Lest thou learn his ways, and get a snare to thy soul (Prov.22:24-25).

If you follow somebody who is angry, it's like following a devil that is tormented.

Farrakhan can only talk about the symptoms and the problems, which is quackery. He has diagnosis without prognosis. But a real doctor, a real practitioner, deals with both diagnosis and the prognosis. He doesn't just make his patients furious over the diagnosis.

Farrakhan is a voice of violent reaction to the injustices in America toward the black man. And misinformed black men are attracted to him because he is charismatic and seems to have an answer.

Many enjoy Farrakhan's philosophy of hate and venom. Farrakhan says, "disorganized love is not as effective as organized hate."[1] And that is an energy, but it is a negative energy.

Angry resentment about slavery or any kind of mistreatment is unproductive. Elsie Robinson says:

> Even if our rage seems fully justified, and our plans succeed beyond our blackest hope, we will never get even. For life doesn't work that way. Instead of finding peace, renewed self-respect, and healing for our hurt, each attempt at revenge leaves us frustrated, cheated. Instead of punishing our enemies, we've simply played our own debasing game and sold ourselves down the river.[2]

You can't live on hate and resentment. But you can live on love, forgiveness, and reconciliation. And if you want to know how much love is willing to give, you have to study the cross. If you want to know how expensive love is, you have to study the cross. If you want to know how far love is willing to go, you have to study the cross.

Christianity deals with love while Farrakhan and Islam deal with the sword, might, and fear. You can live on Christianity's love and forgiveness and reconciliation, but you can't live on hate and resentment, because these are the things that aren't compatible with the soul.

So let's get away from the anger and the resentment. Let's get into the Spirit of God so He can bring about unity and true reconciliation.

Since Martin Luther King died, blacks haven't had a strong voice except for Jesse Jackson. So the news media has made Farrakhan the strong black voice. But he doesn't represent the majority of black men and women in this country — the Nation of Islam has only 20,000 members![3]

Farrakhan may espouse the power that the black man wants, but he says it with anger and venom. There is a vast difference between Louis Farrakhan and Martin Luther King. Martin Luther King was after the same thing, but his method was Christian. He was nonviolent, and he affected change.

The message of the Bible is nonviolent. But Farrakhan's platform is fear. A lot of white people fear him. So do a lot of blacks, because of the threat of reprisal.

Again, Proverbs 22:24-25 says, "Don't follow an angry man." Because if you follow him, you are going to have some trouble. Resentment over slavery or any kind of mistreatment is unproductive. It is living in the past.

No Reparations

Slavery is over; the sentence has been served. And there is no apology necessary — no reparations, no restitution. There is nothing left except, respect.

The black man needs to accept his place in history and move forward into any opportunities to express his gifts and abilities. Demanding or accepting reparations negates the prophecy of God. This implicates man as the source of everything that happened, not God. And all the prophecies disagree with that.

On the ABC program, *Nightline*, Louis Farrakhan recently told Ted Koppel the one billion dollars he wants to accept from Libya was intended as reparations for the Arabs' involvement in the slave trade. But it is wrong to accept reparation money from anyone. God sent the ships. God caused it all because He had a higher purpose in mind — the salvation of many souls.

If any Arab or the white man has to pay, he takes total responsibility for slavery. And that is not accurate. The white man was raised up by God to enslave us idol-worshippers. So all he owes us now is respect.

I encourage any of my fellow blacks reading, instead of looking to others for reparations, look unto Jesus, Who is the author and the finisher of your faith (Heb. 12:2).

No Separatism

Louis Farrakhan is also the strongest voice in the black community today that promotes separatism. And that is a sad step backward. Separatism is an anachronism. It is outdated. It is primitive. It is no longer acceptable. It is not the norm.

Christianity promotes love and unity. So Christianity's answer to Farrakhan is that we are all God's children and that the power of love is greater than the power of hate.

Jesus prayed to His and our Father, "That they [we] may be one, even as we are one" (John 17:22). That certainly doesn't sound like separatism. Separatism divides people. And God is a God of unity, not a God of division.

God doesn't see color as it relates to the spirit of man. He sees our spirits and wants us all together. So if America is going to be the great nation it should be, we will have to be together.

Farrakhan refutes unity's potential. He refutes and argues against the amalgamation philosophy of the United States. But the agape love of God transcends color, it transcends ethnicity, it transcends everything that Farrakhan preaches.

The whole point of Christianity is the challenge of making an enemy into a friend. Christianity has always been positive. It expresses the mind of God, and God is a God of love — agape love. The Bible teaches us to be loving to others who don't deserve to be loved; and receiving love without earning it. Agape love is an extension of grace. It is God's kind of love.

Love doesn't separate; it brings people together. And the church has been given the ministry of reconciliation (2 Cor. 5:18), not a ministry of separatism or division.

No Reverse Racism

I think it is just as bad for blacks to be prejudiced against whites as it is for whites to be prejudiced against blacks. Some groups make white people the creation of the devil; they say white people are low-down, evil demons. Some blacks call white people "honkies" and "rednecks." I used to call them "white niggers" because niggers can be anybody.

But it was wrong to do that. It is venomous. I was just venting my anger because of ignorance. Racism and bigotry are wrong, whichever direction they go.

The Black Muslims count on blacks being racist. They rely on blacks being bigoted. And that is insulting because it is a betrayal of believing the best about our own brothers.

The highest treason is to do the right thing for the wrong reason. Louis Farrakhan espouses hatred for whites. "The Nation [of Islam] teaches that the white race resulted from a botched experiment by a mad black scientist name Yakub."[4]

What Farrakhan espouses — that the black man is god, that he is the only man and that the white man is from the devil — is venomous of racism. To me he is just an opposite color from the white man, because to think that you are superior or you are better than another race is still just racism.

In his book *The End of Racism*, Dinesh D'Souza says,

> Today, Louis Farrakhan continues Elijah Muhammad's tradition of urging blacks in America to awaken to the satanic nature of white, recognize their true pedigree, reclaim their racial heritage, and work with singular purpose to expel the white impostor from his unearned position as master of the universe.[5]
>
> [Farrakhan] now directs his rage toward whites, whom he calls the "mortal enemy."[6]

So, racism is just as bad when the white man practices it, as it is "good" when the black man practices it. D'Souza concludes:

> White racism and black racism are now mirror ideologies, both anchored in relativism and mutually reinforcing. If unopposed, they will surely draw whites and blacks further apart.[7]

Farrakhan wants to be a separate nation within a nation. That's why they call themselves the Nation of Islam. But that's not realistic because he can't provide for forty-eight to fifty million blacks to be a separate nation from the United States.

I would like to say to all the brothers who are embracing Islam and following Farrakhan that he simply doesn't represent the answer. You want an absolute—but Farrakhan isn't it. He doesn't have the answer.

How in the world are we supposed to be a separate country in the United States? Does Farrakhan have any employment for you? You know, a revolutionary must have something to replace the system that he now fights. Does he have a better system than democracy?

I met a man at the airport during the Million Man March, and asked him, "How come, brother, you aren't at the million man march?" He said, "Man, when that march is over, we are still going to have to eat. When Farrakhan can buy Delta Airlines that I work for and hire me, then I will follow him."

Separatism is racism, and racism is evil — no matter who practices it.

Farrakhan Is No Savior

Louis Farrakhan is not my savior, and I hope he is not yours. For him to be my savior, Farrakhan must first have been born by immaculate conception. He would have had to have attained thirty-three years of impeccable living then suffered crucifixion on Calvary's hill. And He would have had to have spoken from the cross, "Father, forgive them, for they know not what they do."

Then he would have had to die. But that's not the hard part. He would then had to have risen on the third day, and he would have to be currently sitting at the right hand of God.

But Louis Farrakhan didn't — and couldn't. And I know the One person who has — my Savior, the Lord Jesus Christ.

Know Who You Are

Two wrongs never make a right. So never dignify someone who does you wrong by becoming like him. Instead, know who you are and be who you choose to be.

If you can't love the root, then you can't love the fruit. A lot of black people don't love themselves because they think they came from the jungle. They don't realize their heritage in the high civilization of Egypt. When you know who you are, you can act responsibly. But when you don't know who you are, anyone can define you. So our true identity comes from God.

Black children at Iowa-Maple School in Cleveland who are being taught their history told Morley Safer of *60 Minutes*, "We came from kings and queens." "We weren't just slaves; we were smart people." And when Safer interviewed the principal, Ms. Bowers-Mosley, she agreed that it was important for the kids to know this "as versus we come from drug dealers."[8]

When you don't love yourself, you can't love anybody else. Jesus said to love your neighbor as you love yourself" (Matt. 19:19). And if you believe you came from the jungle, and that you were a wild animal, you can't love yourself.

Jesus Is the Answer

So again, to all of my brothers — whether at work, or at home, or at church, in jail, on the streets or where ever you may be — I remind you that Jesus said, "I am the way, the truth, and the life: no man cometh unto the Father, but by me" (John 14:6).

Jesus is man enough to cry, but He is God enough to wipe the tears from your eyes. He is man enough to be weary, but He is God enough to say, "Come unto me, all ye that labour and are heavy laden, and I will give you rest" (Matt. 12:28).

Jesus is the manifestation of God in the flesh. He is the Creator Who became the creature. He became dependent so He could be the one that we depend upon.

I tell you, black and white has nothing to do with it. If Jesus was white, he was not white like those who hate you for the color of your skin. If he was black, he was not black like those who steal from, are jealous of, and fight against one another. He is Jesus Christ exclusively.

Jesus Christ represents the lifestyle that is compatible with the soul. The soul is at peace when it is embracing the truth. The truth will make you free; a lie just cannot satisfy.

Love Your Enemies

The truth is in the Bible. The Word of God will change your thinking patterns, if you let it. Now that I know the truth, I view prejudiced white people — the Ku Klux Klan and others involved with racism — as simply uninformed. I see them as people who were vexed by God and need to be delivered by God. And I really believe that when they hear the truth, there is going to be a deliverance.

> There is neither Jew nor Greek, there is neither bond or free, there is neither male nor female; for you are all one in Christ Jesus (Galatians 3:28).

Today I don't react to prejudice as I did before. I can be more objective now rather than subjective. Oh, I'm not perfect in my reactions, but knowing the truth has really changed me from the inside out.

Once you know the Father, you can look at a person with sympathy rather than with disgust. Today I see white men and black men as the same. I would rather be a Christian than to be black or white. Now I can transcend color and see everybody as my brother and my sister.

To Farrakhan I say, "Who is my brother? Who is my sister?" He who does the will of God. So my brother may be white. He may be Russian, German, Czechoslovakian. He may be Shem, Ham or Jepheth.

> For whosoever shall do the will of my Father, which is in heaven, the same is my brother, and sister, and mother (Matt. 12:50).

There are three levels we can choose to live on. The lowest level is to do evil for good. The second level is to do evil for evil. But the highest level is to do good for evil. And this is the level the Christian ought to subscribe to.

If we truly want to be children of our Father in heaven, Jesus told us how:

> Love your enemies, bless them that curse you, do good to them that hate you, and pray for them which despitefully use you, and persecute you; That ye may be the children of your Father which is in heaven: for he maketh his sun to rise on the evil and on the good, and sendeth rain on the just and on the unjust (Matt. 5:44-45).

Christians are called to love all men of all color, no matter how we are treated by them. So let's let go of the quest for justice and move on to this higher level. Yes, brothers, let's move on to healing.

TEN

The Healing of the Black Man

The people who waited at the pool of Bethesda spoken of in John's gospel, and the black man of today, who has been "crippled" as a result of slavery, have a lot in common. Many lie helpless and immobile, knowing where they want to go, but are unable to move where they hope to be.

> Now there is at Jerusalem by the sheep market a pool, which is called in the Hebrew tongue Bethesda, having five porches. In these lay a great multitude of impotent folk, of blind, halt, withered, waiting for the moving of the water. For an angel went down at a certain season into the pool, and troubled the water: whosoever then first after the troubling of the water stepped in was made whole of whatsoever disease he had.
> And a certain man was there, which had an infirmity thirty and eight years (John 5:2-5).

This man waiting at the pool was in an ignominious condition with very little (if any) expectation of change in his life.

> When Jesus saw him lie, and knew that he had been now a long time in that case, he saith unto him, Wilt thou be made whole? (v. 6).

I believe Jesus challenged him, and in paraphrase told him, "Forget about how long you have been here and how many things are against you. Do you want to be made whole? Do you want to get up?"

The impotent man answered him, Sir, I have no man, when the water is troubled, to put me into the pool: but while I am coming, another steppeth down before me (v. 7).

This man was used to his condition to the point of defending it. He had no desire to use his mental ability to defeat the situation, nor did he have the tenacity to chin his way to the pool. In the spirit of confederacy he could have joined with someone else and they could have helped each other to the pool. But he didn't have the initiative to do anything except complain and makes excuses.

This man expostulated and mentally protested that he was not a malinger, one who pretends to be sick to avoid the responsibility of working. And he argued with Jesus that he was legitimately handicapped. But he was more paralyzed in his mind than in his body.

Being made whole has to do with integrity, wholeness of character. A lot of people are physically able, but psychologically they just won't try to improve their situation, because they don't believe they can make it.

Jesus says, "It's your choice. Do you want to get up? That which you have been waiting for, that which troubles the waters to bring healing, is here, talking to you now. You don't have to get in the water. I am here. I am here to heal you."

Victim Consciousness

The man at the pool had a fatal flaw — victim consciousness. He was looking for a comfort zone. Most people who are addicted to alcohol and chemicals want to find a comfort zone. They want to escape reality. Some people even use religion as they would opium. They want a hallucinogenic drug to exempt them from reality.

The worst addiction is "alibi-itis." This addict believes he has fallen and he can't get up, then basks in excuses. He just lies in self-pity, wanting someone to feel sorry for him. Every time he tries to get a job, someone else gets there before him. He doesn't expect to get up because he is too busy blaming somebody else.

76

First he blames the white man. Then, when he gets through blaming the white man, he blames his daddy. He blames his mother. He blames the school system. He blames the church. He blames society.

The black man of today conveniently uses slavery and the injustices of life to justify his lying by the pool.

When a person believes that the system is against him, the white man is against him, and his background is against him, he is a victim with a victim consciousness. He is bogged in many excuses, and will never fulfill his God-given potential, until he gets up.

This kind of victim consciousness makes one prone to leave his family because of polygamy and governmental dependency. It makes one vulnerable to forsake his responsibility as a man.

Dr. Rosie Milligan writes about the condition of the black man:

After Slavery, the pressure was on the black man to support the black woman. Many black men abandoned their families because of the guilt and shame they felt as a result of not being able to provide financially. The Social Service Department would only provide for families not intact.

This is just another form of slavery — being restricted by your condition rather than by chains. Though a man may be physically free, he is not free to perform because the system prevents him from doing so.

In other words, this kind of victim will abandon his family because social services tells him, "We will take care of your family, but you will have to go."

Many Black men abandoned their families because they thought their families would be better off financially with public assistance. As a result of these dilemmas, the Black man began to feel unimportant if he could not provide for his family financially.[1]

So he feels unimportant; he feels less than a man.

Sometimes, he sits down and cries at the humiliation of it all. Sometimes he strikes out at her or the children with his fists, perhaps to lay hollow the claim to being man of the house in the one way that is left open to him, or perhaps simply to inflict pain on this woman who bears witness to his failure as a husband and father and therefore as a man.[2]

Over two-thirds of black babies born in America today are born to single mothers. Where are the fathers?

What group has been documented to show large numbers on drugs, men leaving their families, killing each other, stealing from one another, high unemployment rate, and having affairs outside of marriage?... The world is predicting that, by the year 2000, 70 percent of the Black male seed will be dead, unemployed, or in prison.[3]

Rise and Walk

Jesus saith unto him, Rise, take up thy bed, and walk. And immediately the man was made whole, and took up his bed, and walked: and on the same day was the sabbath (vv. 8-9).

It is time for healing. The failures are over. The defeated way of thinking is in the past. It's time to move on and grow, and to stop making excuses. Jesus never intended for us to remain under the curse of slavery. Jesus is always saying, "Rise and be made whole."

We need black men with strong minds, kind hearts, and willing hands. Men who can be depended on who find joy in labor. Men of courage, honor and strong opinions. Men who have clear minds and high goals who are not afraid of responsibility. Men who are dedicated to a task and are willing to surrender their selfish desires and pursuits to serve.

We need black men of compassion, who are sensitive to the needs of the less fortunate. Men who are tender with their wives and children. Men who have developed an ability to love. Black men need to appreciate the beauties of nature, love their families with passion and honor, and adore womanhood.

When a black man functions effectively as the guide, protector and provider; when his home is ruled with firmness, kindness and love; when security and comfort is provided; when his children become happy, well-adjusted citizens; then he has made his most notable contribution to the world.[4]

It has been said that the sign of a man's success is when he walks up the path to his home and his children run with eagerness to greet him. His wife is smiling and lovingly meets him at the door. This kind of success is not often seen with black men today, but it can be.

Cry Unto God

It's time for the black man to cry unto God. Let's look at the last verses of Isaiah 19 to see how God heals Egypt after He smites it.

> In that day shall five cities in the land of Egypt speak the language of Canaan, and swear to the Lord of hosts; one shall be called, The city of destruction. In that day shall there be an altar to the Lord in the midst of the land of Egypt, and a pillar at the border thereof to the Lord.
>
> And it shall be for a sign and for a witness unto the Lord of hosts in the land of Egypt: for they shall *cry unto the Lord* because of the oppressors, and he shall send them a saviour, and a great one, and he shall deliver them (vv. 18-20).

When the black man cries out unto the Lord because of his oppressions, this is when his healing will start. And now is the time for Egypt — the black people — to cry unto the Lord. You see, it was good that the oppressors came. Because if they hadn't, we would have never cried unto the Lord.

Affliction Makes Way for God's Will

The life of Joseph (Gen. 37-50) is a good example of how God can use affliction to accomplish His will to draw us to Him. Joseph was sold into slavery by his half-brothers. He became a servant in Potiphar's house where Potiphar's wife treacherously lied about him. This led to Joseph's imprisonment, but the Lord was with him there.

While in prison Joseph interpreted the dreams of Pharaoh's chief butler and chief baker, whom Pharaoh had thrown into prison because he was angry with them. Joseph told them both the outcome of their fate. When the butler was exalted to his post again, he forgot about Joseph and left him to languish in prison.

But when Pharaoh had a troubling dream, the butler remembered Joseph and his powers to interpret dreams. So he told Pharaoh, who called Joseph out of prison to interpret his dream. The result was the saving of Egypt from famine, and Joseph was elevated to prime minister over all of Egypt.

As hard as it may sound, if Joseph had never been sold into slavery, he wouldn't have been placed in Potiphar's house. And if he hadn't been in Potiphar's house, Potiphar's wife couldn't have lied about him. And if she hadn't lied about him, he wouldn't have gone to prison. And if he hadn't gone to prison, he wouldn't have met the Pharaoh's baker and butler. And if he hadn't met them, he wouldn't have become prime minister.

So, all things work together for good. God's plan is always right, just as Joseph told his brothers:

> But as for you, ye thought evil against me; but God meant it unto good, to bring to pass, as it is this day, to save much people alive (Gen 50:20).

Joseph looked back on his being sold into slavery, his pain and suffering and imprisonment, and said, "God meant it unto good."

In that way, we can agree with Joseph and with David and say, "It is good for me that I have been afflicted" (Ps. 119:71). If I had not been afflicted, I would have gone astray.

God Brings Healing

And the Lord shall be known in Egypt (v. 21).

It is God's will for the black man to come into the true knowledge of Jesus Christ and out of idol worship so we will sing joyous songs to our Father.

Blacks were world leaders for three thousand years. We aren't in charge now, but God promised to heal us and bring us back to prominence — and He's doing that.

> And the Lord shall smite Egypt: he shall smite and heal it: and they shall return even unto the Lord, and he shall be entreated of

them, and shall heal them (v. 22).

The black man's answer is to be healed from within. If he lays by the pool full of resentment, excuses, and self-pity, and fails to stretch forth his hands unto God, he will die in the problem.

So the way out of the curse of Isaiah's prophecy is to confess with your mouth the Lord Jesus and believe in your heart that God raised Jesus from the dead, and you will be saved (Rom. 10:9). You will be saved from poverty, distress, insecurity, the dread of hell, and from being a paralyzed, inoperative person. Jesus wants you to be a vital person who can make a contribution.

When we go back to God, he will heal us. He did smite us, but now is the time for healing, for being restored to our proper place of health and position.

Confess the Sins of Our Ancestors

Princes shall come out of Egypt; Ethiopia shall soon stretch out her hands unto God (Ps. 68:31).

As blacks, we can't accept the accolades of being descendants of the Egyptians — being pyramid builders and scientists and great leaders — without also accepting the responsibility of the crime of idol worship. So I believe we have to confess not just our sins, but the sins of our ancestors.

God set conditions which the Israelites needed to meet in order to be restored unto Him if they broke His covenants and disobeyed Him:

If they shall confess their iniquity, and the iniquity of their fathers, with their trespass which they trespassed against me, and that also they have walked contrary unto me; And that I also have walked contrary unto them, and have brought them into the land of their enemies; if then their uncircumcised hearts be humbled, and they then accept of the punishment of their iniquity (Lev. 26:40-41).

If the Israelites would do these things, God would remember his covenant with them. So I believe the same is true for us. We must confess the sins of our ancestors to be healed.

81

Be Made Whole

I was once lying by the pool, as an angry victim. But Jesus came and asked, "Wilt thou be made whole?" And when He did, I took the opportunity to receive Him as my Savior.

Now, I have the capacity to love as a result of my metamorphosis in Christ and the agape love of God. The answer for the black man is to get healed and immerse himself in God's agape love, so he can love even his "enemies," and walk on, with head high.

But what about the white man? What is his responsibility? And what about his irritated heart? We will look at this in chapter eleven.

ELEVEN

Prophecy Continued:
The Irritated Heart of the White Man

The black man and the white man are not united in these United States. So far in this writing, we have learned that the black man is under the curse of prophecy until he comes to Christ. But the white man is also the victim of our prophecy: He is suffering from an irritated heart.

> Son of man, take up a lamentation for Pharaoh king of Egypt, and say unto him...I will also vex the hearts of many people, when I shall bring thy destruction among the nations, into the countries which thou has not known" (Ezek. 32:2, 9).

God vexed the heart of the white man in order to execute and fulfill His prophecy on the Egyptians. Just like God vexed the heart of Pharaoh against the Israelites, he vexed the hearts of many against the black man. And today the white man is suffering from a vexed, irritated heart — against the black man.

The Ku Klux Klan and all of those erroneous groups are suffering from irritated hearts. So are many everyday white people. And I believe it's important for the white man to realize that he was not the cause of his irritated heart. I think there is a lot of healing in understanding that God used him as an instrument just as he used Pharaoh as an instrument to enslave Israel. It will allow him to deal with the symptoms of his irritated heart.

The Irritated Heart Defined

Some characteristics of the black man may irritate others. We all experience characteristics in others that are bothersome to us. But if nothing in particular is irritating, the white man is still irritated with the black man, because of his vexed heart. If nothing legitimate justifies his irritation, and he is vengeful and hateful, he has an irritated heart.

For instance, to me Bryant Gumbel is a refined, polished black man. He never gave up his identity as a black man, but he did conform to the system which dictates the acceptable way to be in this country. He never lost his love for his people, and is a man of class who still has the common touch.

Now, if a white person dislikes Gumbel, even though he has adapted and conformed to the system, then the problem is not Gumbel's ability or expertise. The problem stems from the white person's irritated heart.

Precipitous Actions

Some things black people do precipitate reactions; we bring certain things on ourselves. For instance, if a black man walks into a store with a rag tied around his head, pants down, butt out, looking wild and savagelike, he will probably be precipitating a situation where the white man is afraid.

So I am shifting some responsibility back on the black man. If you live a precipitous life, you provoke certain things by your actions and reputation. And there is justifiable cause for the white man to be afraid. But we blacks are just as afraid of such precipitous actions.

Some blacks are trying to move away from other blacks because dead is dead. Whether you're shot by a black man or a white man, the bottom line is that you are dead. And you won't die any better because you were shot by a black man instead of a white man. Dead is dead.

But even without these precipitous characteristics, the irritation against blacks exists in a vexed heart.

Symptoms of an Irritated Heart

Have you ever noticed that *black* has a negative connotation? Black cat, black Sunday, black thoughts. Even the psychology of the pool table reflects this. The cue ball is white and the 8-ball is black. When you sink the 8-ball, you have won the game. If I ever play pool again, I'll switch the cue ball and the 8-ball just for my own satisfaction.

When I grew up, they had an old saying: "If you're white, you're right; if you're brown, stick around; but if you're black, get back." This has been true for hundreds of years.

The white man's irritated heart was revealed through the Europeans who sailed to Africa centuries ago. Once they discovered the value of slaves, they deceived the Africans into believing that their presence there was going to make life better for the Africans. They promised them education and material goods.[1]

Plus, some Africans thought the slaves taken by the white men would be treated as their own slaves were:

> West African slaves enjoyed a status similar to European peasants, in that they often worked their own plots of land, lived in their own towns, and villages, paid tribute to their masters, and held positions of importance in West African societies.[2]

But these Africans had no idea that the white slave trader's vexed heart could allow him to treat these exported African slaves so atrociously. Animals would have been treated better on the slave ships.

Whatever evil you can imagine, it was done to the Africans. Both men and women were raped and used as sex objects. Once in America, slaves who had babies often weren't given enough time off from their constant work to feed them, so they died. Families were torn apart through their sale to different bidders.

Slaves were also tortured and maimed in terrible ways. Some who learned to write had their thumbs cut off. Those who learned to read were killed so they couldn't teach others.

Lynchings were common. Black men and women weren't always just hung; they were also often mutilated and burned. Sometimes parts of their bodies were kept as souvenirs. "Lynching allowed the whites to retain a measure of control by instilling considerable fear among the Black community."[3]

All of these acts of violence and degradation are the result of the prophecy of the white man's irritated heart.

Though black men were given the right to vote in the Fifteenth Amendment that was enacted in 1870 — many measures were taken by the whites to make sure they couldn't vote. Poll taxes were instituted, which were too expensive or that were collected at a specific time and place unknown to the blacks.[4]

Voters in some states were required to read and interpret correctly a section of the state's constitution before they could vote. This even disqualified some whites. Then the grandfather clause was added which exempted all males whose fathers or grandfathers could vote in the January 1, 1867 election from having to take this literacy test. Of course, blacks didn't have the right to vote then, so the grandfather clause exempted just whites.[5]

The "one-drop rule" was created by Virginia legislature in 1924. This law prohibited whites from marrying any person with "a single drop of Negro blood"[6] and shows how the vexed heart went to almost absurd lengths to preserve itself.

It was only three decades ago that blacks were not allowed to eat with whites in certain parts of America. They had their own separate restrooms — or they had none. They had to enter restaurants from the rear if they were allowed in at all. Blacks had to sit in the back of public buses. They couldn't get library cards in their own names.

On a recent television show, a resident from Charleston, South Carolina, told the story about black church life there in the '50s. The free, lighter-skinned blacks went to one church; the darker blacks went to another. And they had what they called a "comb test." If a comb went through the black person's hair easily, he or she was accepted into the lighter-skinned congregation.

This kind of prejudice among blacks came from that same irritated heart of whites. The lighter-skinned blacks knew they were of mixed blood, because they were part white. So they took on the feeling of the superiority of the whites, and their hearts became irritated too.

I saw a white man from Lakeland, Florida, interviewed on another television show recently as he explained how he accosted blacks who were looking for a home in his neighborhood. A couple, a black preacher and his wife, were also interviewed on the show. The white man came out and tried to intimidate them by displaying the confederate flag. He told them that he didn't want any blacks living next to him, and that if they did move in, he would make their lives miserable.

The black family reported this, so the FBI set up a sting operation. They sent a black agent and his wife to the same area. The white man told the undercover FBI agent the same thing. He displayed the confederate flag again and made the same threats. The agent recorded it, and this man was sentenced to jail for twenty-two months.

So we still see overt acts of racism because of the irritated heart of whites. In March 1997 a 13-year-old black boy named Lenard Clark rode his bike into the 99 percent white neighborhood of Bridgeport, Illinois, on his way home from a basketball game. Three white teenagers attacked him, kicking him unconscious, then bragged about taking care of blacks.[7]

Again this act only confirms the fact that the white man's heart is irritated because of Ezekiel's prophecy. God needs to heal him by way of the truth. The white man needs to know that his heart was vexed, because the time is now over for this kind of overt racism and hatred. God will turn on him if he doesn't change.

Blacks aren't going to sit back and tolerate these kinds of acts that are motivated by hatred and do nothing. The fear is gone. There's no room for this anymore.

Covert Racism

But these kinds of overt acts of racism aren't seen that often in our nation today. Because with the exception of the Ku Klux Klan, neo-Nazis and skinheads, most of the racism experienced today is covert.

I'm more concerned about covert racism that overt racism. It's the corporate, church-going irritated white man I'm concerned about, because he masks his irritation with sophistication. You would always rather fight an enemy you can see than one you can't see.

Vexed or irritated hearts contain subtle racism. People don't openly say "Nigger" now. But they may say "welfare queen," or "shiftless," or "lazy." Or they may say "you people," "coons" or "gorillas." And all of these phrases reveal the irritated heart.

People even in the corporate world make sly and iconoclastic remarks against blacks and other races. "You people better be glad that you're over here," they say. The perception is that we're ignorant people and we need to be taught dignity.

People with irritated hearts that God put in them will never be able to relax and cohabitate with the black man. They may tolerate him and work with him, but in the evening, they will get away from him.

In Detroit after 5:00 P.M., the downtown workers leave the city at breakneck speed. The stoplights are synchronized so the corporate world can get out of downtown without any interruption from oncoming traffic from the ghetto. That is a typical sign of the irritated heart.

It's an anachronism now to be a separatist. It's embarrassing to even be associated with low thinkers such as the Ku Klux Klan. But there is a more subtle, sophisticated racism that is going on in the corporate world.

In March of 1997 a federal judge approved a settlement in which Texaco agreed to pay $176.1 million for discriminating against blacks in pay and promotions. A tape of Texaco executives mocking blacks who used terms like, "black jelly beans" further embarrassed Texaco and revealed "a culture still strongly rooted in the commonplace bigotry of turn-of-the-century Texas oilfields."[8]

In 1994 Denny's restaurants agreed to pay $45 million in damages after charges of discrimination against black customers as well as employees came one after another. One Denny's employee was said to have told some black high school kids it was company policy for them to pay for their meals in advance. Then the whole thing blew up when six black Secret Service agents said they were ignored while other officers were served immediately.[9]

So it is very expensive to be a racist in this day and time.

A friend of mine called a well-known hotel after he saw a brochure on it. He asked the hotel manager why no blacks were pictured in the pamphlet as hotel guests, so the manager told him that they would call him back with a response.

The hotel manager thought that he had hung up the phone on his end, but he hadn't. And when my friend heard someone ask the manager who called, the manager replied, "Some black guy wanted to know why we didn't have any blacks in our brochure," to which the other person said, "Why didn't you tell him we couldn't find any? They were all out cleaning chitterlings."

That is the irritated heart of the white man. But your sins will find you out.

In late 1996 the controversy over Ebonics arose. I am personally against Ebonics being used instead of standard English. But I was offended when office fax machines and e-mail boxes around the country began filling up with the following parody (I will only show the parodies that are decent enough to share):

EBONICS - 101

Leroy was an 18-year-old ninth grader. Leroy got an easy homework assignment. All he had to do was to put each of the following words in a sentence. This is what Leroy did:

1. **Foreclose**: If I pay alimony this month, I'll have no money fore-close.

2. **Catacomb**: Don King was at the fight the other night; man, some-body give that catacomb.

3. **Disappointment**: My parole officer tol me if I miss disappoint-ment, they gonna send me back to the big house.

4. **Israel**: JJ tried to sell me a rolex; I said man, that looks fake. He said no israel.

5. **Stain**: My mother-in-law axed if I was stain for dinner again.

6. **Seldom**: My cousin gave me two tickets to the knicks game so I seldom.

No law can legislate love. You can't legislate fellowship. It has to come as the result of a circumcision of the heart. The white man's heart must be made right. He must recognize that he is not the only kid on the block.

Not All Hearts Are Vexed

The Bible says that the heart of *many* will be vexed; it doesn't say *all*. John Brown, Abraham Lincoln, and others, were men enough to stand for the abolition of slavery.

Rev. John Newton was convicted by the Holy Spirit because he knew it was humanity on those ships, and he got converted as a result of God touching him. In his later years, he fought strongly to abolish the slave trade, even writing a pamphlet in 1788 against slavery, *Thoughts Upon the African Slave Trade*.

We also need to remember that even during the civil rights move-ment, many whites died because their hearts were not vexed.

So God did not vex all the hearts of people.

Healing for the Vexed Heart

Just as it's hard to believe God would allow the black people to suf-fer so, it's hard to believe that God would put a vexed heart that is so horrendous in white people. But he did it to execute punishment. He raised up the white man and vexed his heart because He hates sin. If He was willing to sacrifice His own Son to take away the sins of the world,

He would surely raise up a terrible slave master to drive sin out of a people.

For those whose hearts are irritated, there is healing available. God used the irritated heart as an instrument to punish the idolaters of Egypt. He is the One Who can remove the irritated heart, through Jesus Christ.

TWELVE

The Healing of the White Man

———

So, we have learned how God raised up the white man to fulfill the prophecies of enslavement and of the scattering of the idolatrous Egyptians among the nations. But when God says that the chastisement is over, and that the sentence is completed, and the release date has come, it is wrong for the instrument whom God raised up to continue to execute sentence.

When someone goes to jail and does his time, it's not lawful to hold him longer than his sentence. This is what God is saying to the white man. If the white man continues to dominate and oppress the black man, God can turn on him.

So it's time for those with irritated hearts to release them to God and be healed. Racism and separatism are out of step with the times and out of step with God. So is the white system — a system with just whites in control. Therefore, God is now against the white man's heart continuing to be vexed against the black man.

The Chastisement Is Over

Look at the example of Pharaoh. God hardened his heart because He was setting Pharaoh up to destroy him. He got him in the Red Sea, swallowed up his army, and finished his power. You don't want that. So the best thing to do is to let go of all this subtle racism that's not Christian.

In 2 Chronicles 28 we find the story of God delivering Ahaz, king of

Judah, and his people into the hands of the king of Israel. These two peoples were brethren who had been divided. The people of Israel slew many of Ahaz's men. Then they took captive two hundred thousand people of Judah — men, women and children. But a prophet of God, Obed, said to the people of Israel:

> Behold, because the Lord God of your fathers was wroth with Judah, he hath delivered them into your hand, and ye have slain them in a rage that reacheth up unto heaven. And now ye purpose to keep under the children of Judah and Jerusalem for bondmen and bondwomen unto you: but are there not with you, even with you, sins against the Lord your God?
>
> Now hear me therefore, and deliver the captives again, which ye have taken captive of your brethren: for the fierce wrath of the Lord is upon you (vv. 9-11).

Just as Israel was used by God to punish Judah for idolatry, the white man was used to punish the black man for idolatry. But when the punishment was over, God warned the people not to overdo it. Otherwise the fierce wrath of God would come upon them. And the people of Israel obeyed:

> And the men...took the captives, and with the spoil clothed all that were naked among them, and arrayed them, and shod them, and gave them to eat and to drink, and anointed them, and carried all the feeble of them upon asses, and brought them to Jericho, the city of palm trees, to their brethren (v. 14).

Israel heeded the warning to stop. And they did more than stop; they applied healing balm to the physical, emotional, and spiritual wounds.

The white man must accept the fact that Jesus is the Christ of all nations, and that healing will come as a result of hearing the truth. The truth of the matter is, the white man was the instrument, but now the expiration date has come. Slavery is over, and a multicultural society is everywhere.

The white man must receive the fact that God loves Egypt — those who were enslaved — and that He loves Assyria — those who did the enslaving. God is a God of all nations; His temple is a house of prayer for all nations.

Slavery was God's form of chastisement to bring blacks out of idol worship to the true and living God. But now that this task has been complete, we need to move on, loving with agape love, which does not act unseemly. And as we do, that's when the healing will come.

A Changed Heart Through Jesus Christ

In Jesus there is no bond, there is no slave, there is no Jew, no Greek (Col. 3:8). In Jesus we all have been delivered from the curse of the law, because Jesus became the curse for us (Gal. 3:13).

> There is therefore now no condemnation to them which are in Christ Jesus, who walk not after the flesh, but after the Spirit (Rom. 8:1).

Jesus represents the absolute answer. He is in the business of raising up men, whether they be white or black. He is an equal-opportunity Deliverer. And He will deliver anybody — from failure to success, from death to life, from wrong to right.

The knowledge of the truth will deliver those who have irritated hearts.

> He sent his word, and healed them, and delivered them from their destructions (Ps. 107:20).

All divine healing comes as a result of the truth — God's Word — being received into hearts.

A circumcision of the heart comes as a result of the truth.

Even after we come under the "new management" of the Holy Spirit, we have to pray that the old man will become dysfunctional to be put out of business. So don't entertain those old thoughts. Resist the devil.

> Casting down imaginations, and every high thing that exalteth itself against the knowledge of God, and bringing into captivity every thought to the obedience of Christ (2 Cor. 10:5).

93

Brother Strengthening Brother

I was once full of resentment and venom. I felt justified in believing that the white man was the enemy who must be fought. I believed that truth and justice would prevail, and that the enemy would soon be destroyed.

But now I have been converted like Peter. Do you know that Peter had a problem with prejudice, too? Yes, he did. Peter was very prejudiced against anybody who wasn't a Jew. So Jesus used a vision to tell him not to call unclean that which is clean in God's sight. (See Acts 10).

Because of the truth of God's Word and the Holy Spirit, the white man is now "clean" in my sight.

And as Jesus told Peter, "When thou art converted, strengthen thy brethren" (Luke 22:32), I feel this message is much the same. (See Acts 15:8-9).

Now that I am converted, I'm not pro black or pro white. I'm pro Christ; I'm pro Christian. I'd rather be Christian than white. I rather be a Christian than black. Now I am willing to strengthen my white brother and say to him, "Let's move on to maturity. Let's make the cultural issue no issue, and color and the differences no difference."

Deliverance from the curses of Egypt's prophecy is freedom for both blacks and whites. The whites are free from the vexed heart. The blacks are free from the chastisement. So we can become brothers — working together and helping each other.

And this should occur first in the Church — the body of Christ. So in the next chapter we will see how we're doing.

THIRTEEN

Healing in the Church

In late 1996 I saw a television news program about a predominately white church that had a black pastor assigned to it. After he was there a while, the church went black because the Afro-centric style of worship was not accepted by whites.

One white couple said they couldn't get with the black style of worship. The reporter also interviewed the minister, who cried during the taping. He felt rejected and sad at the turn of events.

On the other hand, The Rock of Our Salvation Church in Chicago is 65 percent black and 35 percent white. Its pastor, Raleigh Washington, reveals a key to moving toward unity:

> We must deliberately increase our sensitivity and gain knowledge to relate empathetically with our brothers and sisters of different backgrounds.[1]

So you know this Chicago area church isn't going to allow their cultural differences to separate them any longer.

Flavoring for the Gospel

The Gospel is like a piece of meat that can be flavored in many different ways. And each particular flavoring brings out the personality of the cook. I see the preacher as a cook; his style depicts his personality, or his ethnicity. Truth needs personality, just like chicken needs seasoning.

In the black community you have fried chicken and smothered chicken. Then there is New Orleans Cajun chicken, Italian chicken cacciatore, Mexican chicken mole, and so on. Each one of the flavors represents an aspect of the same chicken. So I can put my flavoring into the message — and so can you.

The Black Flavor

Maya Angelou wrote a book about the black experience, *I Know Why the Caged Bird Sings*. In it she says the cage gave the bird a song, a song of hope. Slavery and everything that the black people have gone through has given us a soul full of expression that even white people enjoy.

In Washington, DC, there is a black restaurant called the Florida Grill where all the legislators and big shots from the Hill go. I've been there a couple of times, and I have noticed how the white men relish the smothered chicken, rice and beans, collard greens, and candied yams.

When we add our personalities and our cultural flavors, we can experience and enjoy each other.

The world knows how to capitalize on the black man's rich culture. In music, for instance, James Brown, Ray Charles, Michael Jackson, Elvis Presley, the Beatles, Li'l Richard — have all developed musical styles rooted in the black culture. The world knows how to capitalize on what is culturally beautiful and artistically wonderful about the black people and has mastered the mixing. So why can't the church wake up to this realization?

If churches have different styles of worship, there shouldn't be a conflict. We should be able to come together and an enjoy the difference. That's maturity.

It's like eating a meal — there's a time for appetizers, a time for the main course, and a time for dessert. We can't just eat salad. In the black church, we build in worship from soft, slow songs to a loud, climactic experience. There has to be a point of climax, so we build to that.

We can teach the white man how to yadah, todah, shebach and shout hallelujah, rave and lose your mind, so to speak, and to have a fit for God.

The black church has been accused of being too emotional, and the white church has been accused of being too starchy and quiet. There ought to be a balance of being didactic while yet explosive — combining mental acceptance along with emotional involvement.

Helping Each Other

Blacks often go to white churches because they are tired of the petty bickering and the lack of organization in the black church. They go to the white church seeking peace, because sheep love to dwell beside still waters.

Blacks are constantly warring against one another in churches for no apparent reason. We often sell our birthright for a position of status in the church. Then the question often arises of where all the money goes. All *what* money?... I'd like to know.

Blacks fight black leadership, so black church leaders can't get respect as God's men. Yet blacks will leave the black church to go to the white church and submit. They pay tithes without being coerced. They give offerings to the white preacher without his having to beg for them.

The way we blacks are blatantly disobedient to church leadership reveals the remnants of the prophecy left on us. Don't ever make a member angry or remove him or her from a position, because that person won't be satisfied until he or she has destroyed the whole church by sowing discord throughout it. Yet that same person will go to a white church and be as humble and submissive as a lamb.

The fact that the black pastor may appear blessed because he lives in a nice house, drives a nice car, and wears nice clothes, irritates some of the black parishioners. We say we love our brothers and sisters who are successful, but without repentance and real salvation, our hearts are yet jealous.

I believe whites ought to come to black churches because it will bring social, racial and economic balance. There is a cultural advantage to both blacks and whites dwelling together in unity. It is then that we will understand what true agape love is all about.

Blacks have always migrated toward whites, whether it be to their women, to their church, or to their neighborhoods. The trend now, it seems, is that the successful black has a tendency to join white churches rather than their own black churches. Because you see, the white man sets a standard to what seems to be the best. So blacks going to white churches has never been a problem, but whites going to black churches has.

This is reflected in our cities as well. The whites live in the suburbs, and the blacks are in the city. That's the way it is in the churches, too. The eleven o'clock hour is still the most segregated hour in our country just as Martin Luther King said because we haven't learned how to accept the differences and to make no difference out of the difference.

One culture should help another. Every culture brings something to the table that is an embellishment for the other. What are we going to do when we get to heaven? I don't think there will be a black section and a white section, or a white choir and a black choir.

We need to respect one another here and now — that is the equivalent to love.

Racism in the Church

I had an unpleasant encounter with racism in the '70s in Los Angeles when I preached at a church that was predominantly black but had a white leader. I noticed the black people would come to church on time and give money, but they were illiterate, and nobody there was trying to educate them.

I asked one of the black ministers if any blacks worked in the office. He said they weren't allowed in the office. So I decided I would never again preach for a white man who had a predominantly black congregation because it was nothing but religious slavery.

I was hoping I could see the head pastor privately. I probably would have told him some things, hoping to upset him so I could stage a protest. *If this is Christianity, something is wrong*, I thought.

Another bad experience I had with racism among Christians happened at a National Religious Broadcaster's (NRB) convention I attended in the '80s.

I went with a Bishop from the Church of God in Christ who wanted me to see how the white people do things. That bothered me because I wasn't yet delivered from my anger toward whites. And I wondered, *Did he think white people did things better than we did*?

At the convention they put all the black preachers in a separate room to discuss black ministries. In this room was a microphone that was discovered to be carrying our conversation to another room where white people were recording the discussion.

Bishop Ithiel Clemmons, who is now a board member of the Church of God in Christ, took issue with that. He became very upset, and got on the microphone to tell the NRB people that he didn't appreciate what they were doing. The meeting should have either been private or integrated. But as it was set up, it was demeaning and sneaky.

I was angry almost to the point of throwing chairs. Why did they put us off in a room as though we were separate? The Bishop I was with didn't see anything wrong with it, but I was furious.

A prominent black minister was slated to be the speaker the next afternoon, and Rev. Billy Graham was slated to speak that night. The black minister had bused in over one hundred members of his choir. Yet his message was very poorly attended. There were more choir members than attendees there. The audience was mostly black, with one table of whites.

This minister resorted to a style of preaching that would have been appropriate at his home church — that we call squalling. It is the equivalent to singing your message. It is acceptable in the black church because it is a way of celebrating, a way of maximizing our energy and seasoning the message. It is a very demonstrative style.

But the table of white people left when he started squalling, right in the middle of the man's message. I was angry at them for being so disrespectful, and I was angry at him for not being able to adapt to a different audience. The blacks were rooting for him and praising him and giving him the kind of support he needed and wanted at that time. But he seemed to me like an Uncle Tom, begging for acceptance. He was an NRB board member, yet the people showed that this man was nothing more than a token by not coming to hear him speak.

That night Rev. Billy Graham spoke in the same room, and the place was jammed. I love Rev. Billy Graham, but the disparity was so obvious that I actually cried. It was the first time in my life I cried about racism. I was so upset, I was ready to go out and grab somebody. The irritated hearts of these white Christians were revealed.

I said I'd never go back. I didn't want anything to do with white ministries or white preachers. It was a time of personal setback for me and I decided to stay in the safe haven of the Church of God in Christ, away from whites. I'm not saying I was right to be angry. Now I know that the heart of the white man was irritated by God. But we need to take a long, hard look at racism and prejudice in the body of Christ.

Facing Our Sins

Cry aloud, spare not, lift up thy voice like a trumpet, and shew my people their transgression, and the house of Jacob their sins (Is. 58:1).

We must all talk about our sins in the body of Christ in order to fix them.

For the time is come that judgment must begin at the house of God: and if it first begin at us, what shall the end be of them that obey not the gospel of God? (1 Pet. 4:17).

We have to start the healing process in the church. Because if we as Christians can't succeed at this with the Holy Spirit's help, what hope is there for the world?

The fact that the white man was not responsible for slavery takes away his false guilt. But he must be honest before God. He must eradicate any prejudice and racism because the sentence has been served. It's over.

The fact that God sent the ships means that the black man must let go of his anger toward whites. He must repent of his ancestors' sins and his own resentment toward whites. Then we can have healing and closure. Then we can start to work together as one body — one body of Christ.

The Color of Love

We have to ask the question: What is the color of love? Is it black? Is it brown? Is it white? No, the color of Love is red because Jesus loved us and gave His life for us.

What is the color of justice? It is red. People died in wars so they could bring about a democracy of equality.

If you want to know how much love is willing to give, you have to study the cross. If you want to know how far love is willing to go, you have to study the cross. If you want to know how expensive love is, you have to study the cross.

We have to get beyond the color thing and get to the real issue of love. And love doesn't mean apologizing for things you didn't cause.

FOURTEEN

No Apology Necessary, Just Respect

A t this point of our discussion, it should be well established that a crime was committed. The criminal was arrested. He was brought before the judge and sentenced. Then he was incarcerated for a certain period of time. But now his sentence has been served. Should the criminal feel that the arresting officer must apologize for arresting him? No. Should he feel that the judge who sentenced him must apologize? No. And neither should the guards at the jail.

The white man was just the arresting officer, he was only God's instrument. So the white man owes us no apology, just respect.

God's method has always been to raise up one nation to enslave another who had turned against Him. No one could have cursed us unless God had cursed us first (Num. 23:8). No one could have enslaved us unless God had authorized it.

Just an Instrument of God

A friend of mine, Charles Brown from New Orleans, once told me a story about a little fellow in day care. This little guy would act up, then apologize and say that he was sorry. But he would keep doing the same thing over and over. Charles pointed out that sometimes sorry is not enough. Because sorry is what sorry does. Sorry has to do with repentance and change of attitude. So in the conversation Charles said that if the white man was really sorry, he would prove it in his actions. I

101

agreed, but I challenged him on his premise.

"Do we really want him to say that he is sorry?" I asked. "Should he be sorry if he is just an instrument?"

If the white man should apologize to us for enslaving us four hundred years, then we, the blacks, should apologize to Israel for enslaving them four hundred years. Four hundred years — for four hundred years.

There's a fine line between accepting responsibility for being a slave master and accepting the fact that you were the instrument. The white man needs to decide whether he was the instrument or the one who orchestrated the whole thing, and I'm trying to get him off the hook.

Promise Keepers

There is a movement in the body of Christ, mainly focused in Promise Keepers, that feels a need to apologize to blacks for slavery. They use the Scripture, "Confess your faults one to another, and pray one for another, that ye may be healed" (James 6:16). But I believe this idea is somewhat lopsided because the white man is doing all the apologizing. It's easy for the black man to relish the idea, but the truth is that God was behind the slavery. He sent the ships, and He takes full responsibility for His acts.

Believe me, apologies are good, but truth is so much better. When we fully understand that God was behind our enslavement, and that God vexed the heart of the white man against us, then no apology is necessary. I believe the hearts of the people leading Promise Keepers are in the right place. They are seeking reconciliation. But by taking on the burden of apologizing for slavery, I believe they are taking on a responsibility that isn't theirs.

Apologizing says to the black man that the white man orchestrated slavery because of greed, imperialism, superiority and so forth. It takes away from the truth of prophecy, and it further implies that slavery occurred with God having nothing to do with it. God is saying to me that He doesn't want anybody to take responsibility for what He has done. If we look to the white man as the culprit and the villain, then we imply that God didn't have anything to do with it. And God is too big a God to allow anybody to take the blame for something He did.

A white man couldn't make this statement; it has to come from within the black race. I know this will rock a whole lot of foundations and that it is full of *skandalizo* — that is, the ability to offend. But it is the truth. And to know better is to do better. The motivation to want reconciliation is good. But in order to have absolute reconciliation, it's imperative to have absolute truth. Then we can have real healing and closure. The only thing that is going to heal us is absolute truth. "Ye shall know the truth, and the truth shall make you free" (John 8:32). We must get a healing and move on.

I think Promise Keepers is doing a good job, but they need absolute truth. As long as you don't know the truth, you will continue to apologize. I've talked to some of our black clergy who are tired of receiving it. And I'm sure white people are tired of apologizing.

There is no closure in apologizing, because there's always another white person who should apologize and another black person who should receive it. But they keep on apologizing because there is no closure. This could go on indefinitely, even though everyone wants to get on to the next step.

I believe Promise Keepers is acting out of well-meaning ignorance. Even though it is noble and politically correct, it is biblically wrong. They are striving to bring about unity, but unless there is a healing, the white heart will remain irritated and the black man will remain exempt from his responsibility of having committed a crime. I believe that knowing the truth can bring real closure, so we can all go on to real fellowship. This is a hard pill to swallow, but it's a necessary pill.

The Importance of Respect

So, if the white man was just the instrument, we must face the reality that we committed a crime, and the crime was idol worship. For our crime we were incarcerated four hundred years. But the sentence is complete, the time has expired. We have been set free. And what we need now is respect — not apologies.

The time is here for the white man to respect his brother the black man. Respect means accepting the differences of those living in a multicultural society. Respect engenders acceptance. You don't necessarily have to like a person to respect a person. If we are born again, we can love with agape love. So we have the power through God to accept others because we have the heart of God.

In his book *Makes Me Wanna Holler*, Nathan McCall deals with respect. He was in jail as a young man but then went on to college to get a degree in journalism. After he graduated, he landed a job with a newspaper in Norfolk, Virginia. But even though he was educated and able to compete with the paper's white journalists, he didn't feel their respect. There was always the suggestion that whites were superior. He was relegated to menial jobs like covering certain things in the black community that no one thought were important, and he wanted to work in the mainstream culture.

In his book, McCall explains how respect is paramount to the black man. The black man will kill for respect because he feels he has been disrespected for four hundred years:

> For as long as I can remember, black folks have had a serious thing about respect. I guess it's because white people disrespected them so blatantly for so long that blacks viciously protected what little morsels of self-respect they thought they had left.... It was universally understood that if a dude got disrespected, he had to do what he had to do.[1]

Blacks kill other blacks because of disrespect. Some say, "It's bad enough that the white man disrespects me, but I'm not going to take that from you."

McCall points out that in the black community, gangs fight one another for respect, and that once the respect is gained, the fight is over. Even on the basketball court they play for respect. They don't play for money — but for respect.

My brother was an excellent fighter, and I was his protégé. He was my hero because he was the "baddest" fighter in the neighborhood. I just loved to see him box, because he usually won. He would even fight men who were double his age and twice his size. And if he didn't beat them, he would never give up until they respected him. He would say when the fight started, "Bring your lunch because we are going to be here for a while."

To me that was a great thing — my brother wasn't going to quit until he got respect. He would fight for respect, even if he lost. He eventually went to the reformatory, and I followed later. But by the time I got there, his reputation was already established. Everybody there respected the name Carter because my brother fought for that respect. And I had to maintain that respect by fighting, but I enjoyed the fact that my brother's reputation had proceeded me. It gave me a sense of pride.

You may think I had pride in the wrong thing and for the wrong reasons. But the facts remain! Black men need respect, and they will do anything to get it. This desperate need may seem trivial to the white man because he has always had respect. But respect is a big thing in the black community.

The Nation of Islam leader Louis Farrakhan preaches that black men are suffering from a lack of appreciation and respect. So let's give blacks the respect they deserve so they won't resort to following violent men like him to get it.

Showing Respect Through Titles

In the black community guys have different nicknames. In my neighborhood in Charleston, for instance, guys had names like Bell Pepper and Tater Bud and Tough Man, and they fought for them because they became legendary names in the black community. They were a source of pride and respect.

As a black man, I never had the acceptance and validation that comes with any position. When you reduce me to the rank of "Brother," that's my entry level experience with Jesus — being born again. When I got into the ministry, and now having ministered for nearly thirty years, I think you should not hold me to that level of Brother. Now that I have a small position in the ministry from the Lord, I would like to be respected for it and called by my title, Reverend or Pastor.

People in the white church are on first name basis, but in the black church we believe in protocol because we've never had it. Blacks address men as Mr., Reverend, Pastor, Elder or Bishop, and some whites use, Brother, for everyone.

I want to be respected by my ecclesiastical peers because of my position. I am respected as a husband and father by my wife and my children. And I want respect from other men because I am a man.

I once saw a young preacher on TV refer Rev. Billy Graham as, "Billy," when talking about a meeting he had with Rev. Graham. I thought that was disrespectful of him, a young minister, to address a great preacher who has been such a man of integrity and a towering hero as, "Billy."

When you address a black man, the greatest thing you can do for him is to use his title. Call him Dr., or Pastor, or just call him Mr. Smith. Give him that respect because he needs it. If his name is Henry Smith, call him Mr. Smith, because he's never had that acceptance and respect before. The black man simply wants respect from the white man, just as he wants it from his woman, because he's been without it for so long.

I remember the greatest feeling in the world I ever had with my father was when he made a white man respect him. I remember that day so well. My father worked for a bakery. One day he and I were delivering bread to this exclusive restaurant, and the man who received deliveries said something like, "How are you doing, George, my boy?" I don't think he meant any harm, it didn't sound demeaning anyway. But my father, at the expense of possibly losing the account said, "How old do you have to be to be called a man? You called me a boy in front of my son." Then my father, who was a tough guy made that man apologize, and said, "Do not, as long as you live, ever address me like that."

Proper Protocol

Today people don't use "Boy" too much, but most do address one another on a first name basis, and that is disrespectful to us too. White people go to church dressed very casually. No protocol. They go to the baseball game dressed the same way they dress for church. There's got to be a difference between the palace and the baseball field.

Respect Our Culture

Sometimes whites overcompensate. For instance, a bishop friend of mind told me about the time in the '50s when he visited a white church and the pastor acknowledged him by saying, "Now we are going to show that we love our Brother. We want everybody to line up and we are going to kiss our Brother." That was really going overboard. Black people just want to be accepted.

But even if you don't accept me, I demand that you respect me, because I wasn't born in some jungle. My beginning like everyone else's on earth had its origin in Adam, and I am also the descendant of Pharaohs, kings and queens, because of my lineage from Ham. My people built the pyramids of Egypt. We were important world leaders for three thousand years, but we made a mistake. We aren't a people who were down and are on our way up; we were people that were up, but were taken down and are now on our way back up. So respect me for my history. Respect me for my ability, respect me for the fact that I am your brother and that we are all in the body of Christ.

In a multicultural society, no culture has the right to insult and criticize another. The black man is the only one who can criticize his own people. That is why I, a black man, am saying these things — explaining our sin of idolatry.

Some time ago a white preacher on television infuriated me because he was trying to tell black people who to choose as their leader. He said Jesse Jackson was the wrong person to look to as a leader of the black people. That may be true, but this white man wasn't qualified to pick our leaders. It is wrong for whites to choose for or criticize the black culture.

I see a lot of criticism of the black culture. We are different. We have suffered. Because of that, we have a different form of expression. We maximize our energy; we're explosive, emotional people. And that shouldn't be criticized, it should be enjoyed. We taught the world how to sing. We taught the world how to dance. And we taught the world how to enjoy themselves, even in poverty. We have a buoyancy to bounce back, and a tremendous tenacity to persevere. So we need to be respected for that.

Politics of Acceptance

The philosopher Thomas Hobbes (1588-1679), who studied the ways of man, wrote that the state of human nature is *to accept the few, never the masses.* Hobbes claimed that people accept individuals based on education, financial status and gifts (talents).Whites and blacks both think like that.

Let me give you an example. Sammy Davis and Frank Sinatra were tight — close friends. On one occasion when they were playing in the same city, Sammy Davis went over to the club where Frank Sinatra was to see him, but they wouldn't let him in because he was black. Of course Mr. Sinatra, the "Chairman of the Board," fixed that right away and made club management let Sammy Davis come in and sit anywhere he wanted.

Frank Sinatra respected Sammy Davis for his ability. He may not let every other black into his circle because of human nature's tendency to accept the few. But because that is true, you can only deduce that Hobbe's politics of acceptance is that you eliminate the ungifted and those who aren't privileged financially and so forth in accepting the few. Some people will accept me now because of what I drive and where I live. Why couldn't they accept me before?

Years ago before I was changed in my heart I went into an upscale men's clothing store in Philadelphia looking for a white Italian suit. I wasn't dressed properly because I was just getting off work, but my pocket was full of money.

I told the salesman, "I'd like to have a nice white double-breasted suit. No vents — I like the Italian cut." But the salesman judged me based on my apparel and my black skin, and he took me over to the inferior cheap suits.

"Is this all you have?" I asked.

The salesman hedged, and said, "I guess so. The others cost a lot of money."

So I told him, "I hope you aren't judging me because of the color of my skin or what I'm wearing. I want to see your best suits." He hesitated a little bit, so I dismissed him. I told him not to even come near me. Then I went to the manager and told him I didn't want that salesman near me. So another salesman was assigned who took me to the very expensive Italian suits and I bought the suit with cash.

I also bought a pair of shoes. I just went on an extravagant shopping spree. Then I told the first salesman, "Next time you see any man, black or white, don't judge him by the color of his skin or by the apparel he is wearing. Let this be a lesson to you." I was able to gain respect after I had been misjudged.

Even if human nature is to accept a few, never the masses, we need to become like Jesus, Who said, "Come unto me all you who labor and are heavy laden, and I will give you rest" (Matt. 11:28). Because Jesus accepted the masses.

But I have discovered that when I'm carnal and not walking in the Spirit, I have the tendency to block people out of my circle. Sometimes it's for my safety, and sometimes it's because of my inward discrimination against others. I find myself not wanting to have certain people in my circle because they aren't dressed properly or are hygienically challenged. That's our human nature, but it isn't the Holy Spirit's nature.

E Pluribus Unum means "Out of Many, One." That's the strength of the United States. Coming together and letting the strong bear the infirmities of the weak. We must never throw anybody away. The answer to the problem of racial discrimination is to accept every man no matter what his condition. And that can come with Christian maturity. Because Jesus loved everybody, we need to grow into that. So in the next chapter we will conclude this writing by looking at how we must all come together — to work as one.

FIFTEEN

Coming Together

———

God has given each race that came from His hand His creative ability. Each has strengths, and each has weaknesses. We're like puzzle pieces with gaps for others to fit into. Remember that the nations originated from Noah's three sons. The descendants of Ham built the great pyramids of Egypt. It does my heart good to know that the Egyptians were builders and inventors. Don't you know that they would be astounded with the inventions of our day, such as airplanes, cars, and telephones.

The descendants of Japheth also made great contributions to mankind. And of course, through Shem came the Old Testament prophets and our Savior, Jesus Christ. The point to be made is that in a multicultural society we need to respect our differences and make no difference out of the differences. We all need each other.

Andrew J. Beard, a black railroad worker, designed a railroad car coupling in the late 1800s.[1] But what good was that without a train? See, we need each other. Another black man, Granville T. Woods, invented the automatic stop sign, and sold the patent to General Electric in 1923.[2] But what good was Beard's stoplight without the car the white man invented?

So we need each other. We need to accept one another on the basis of our character rather than the superficiality of color. We need to accept and respect each other and love each other — because love is the answer.

Healing and Restoration

In this book we have looked at the terrible prophecies that were spoken against Egypt in Isaiah 19. Now, let's look at the conclusion of that chapter. Because after chastisement comes healing and restoration:

> In that day shall there be a highway out of Egypt to Assyria, and the Assyrian shall come into Egypt, and the Egyptian into Assyria, and the Egyptians shall serve with the Assyrians (v. 23).

It is important to keep in mind that Assyria was used by God to enslave the Egyptians, just as the white man was used to enslave the blacks in recent history. But Isaiah's prophecy also shows that all those animosities will be put to rest in a coming time when there will be a multicultural existence, with everyone freely moving and working together.

Because God never intended for us to be by ourselves. He loves all cultures and races, and wants us to work together.

> In that day shall Israel be the third with Egypt and with Assyria, even a blessing in the midst of the land: Whom the Lord of hosts shall bless, saying, Blessed be Egypt my people, and Assyria the work of my hands, and Israel mine inheritance (vv. 24-25).

Noah's three sons went their separate ways, but here in Isaiah's prophecy, we see them brought together again. Blacks and whites — once enemies — are bound together with Israel, salvation from God, being the binding force.

So we can come together. I'm not for separatism anymore. The black community must recognize that God wants us to coexist with Assyria (the oppressor), through Israel (Jesus). God wants unity. He wants harmony. He wants us working together as one.

If Christianity is really working, the people of God will make an enemy a friend. That's what happened to Gloria Busch Johnson, a black woman, and Robert Funk, a white man.

Gloria grew up in South Carolina in the days when whites and "coloreds" had separate public bathrooms. She was a civil-rights marcher, who endured being spat on and hosed down in the spirit of passive resistance. Robert was a white man who grew up with blacks as friends, but who became prejudiced later in life.

Robert joined the police force in South Carolina and participated in the breaking up of civil-rights marches. He resolved in his heart that he didn't want anything to do with blacks — ever. Then over the course of time, both Gloria and Robert became Christians. When Robert later contracted chest pains, he went to an evangelistic meeting at the urging of his wife. But when the speaker pointed him out and told him God wanted to heal him, he also pointed out Robert's racism and that he needed to get his life straightened out. From that point on, Robert prayed that God would change his heart. He knew it was something he would have to work on.

Then one day Gloria walked into the church Robert was attending and she gave the usher, who happened to be Robert, a big hug. Robert stiffened up, and Gloria noticed. So she decided she would keep working on him, and the next several Sundays, she did the same thing.

Gloria and Robert's wife Beverly became friends. And when Robert and Beverly started having some marital problems, Beverly asked him if Gloria, who was a counsellor, could talk with them. Robert finally opened up to her, and she gave him some counseling that really helped the marriage. And before long Gloria and Robert also became friends.[3]

We can't be separate in the United States. Being separate is anachronism, a relic from the past. Change can begin with spiritual awakening. So let's forget the past. Unless we live together, we will all be destroyed together. The answer is to be born of the Spirit and to grow in God's Word. Because when we are born of the Spirit, love will not offend my brother. Love covers a multitude of faults.

Something to Talk About

The story is recorded in John 4 about how a Samaritan woman was ministered to by Jesus after His disciples went into town to buy food. Culturally, Jews had no dealings with the Samaritans. They were considered to be dogs. But this Jew was different.

Jesus was one Jew Who wouldn't discriminate against this woman. He showed agape love in their encounter. And all of that gave her something to talk about, so she went into town and told everyone about Jesus.

Like Jesus, we all need to give the world something to talk about.

It was in Antioch that believers were first called "Christians". It was actually a term of derision. But oh, that we would have the honor to be accused of being Christlike enough to love our brothers in spite of their color; to go out of our way to express the altruism of practical Christianity; to mingle with each other without making distinctions and without covert racism.

Let's give the world something to talk about. Let's go eat at one another's houses and worship at one another's churches, just as Gloria Johnson and Robert Funk did. Let's picnic together. Let's allow our sons and daughters to know and care about each other.

Let's give them something to talk about.

Let's be accused of being people who will stand by each other and help each other, who will forgive each other and pray for each other and live for each other and be like Jesus.

On the day of Pentecost, all the people got together to hear what God was doing — the Parthians, the Medes, the Mesopotamians, the Judeans, the Egyptians, the Libyans, the Romans, and the Arabians (Acts 2:9-11). The Holy Ghost is the only one who can bring about unity. Let's let Him do it.

Let's live our faith so we can light up the world. Then when the world sees the light of the Gospel in our character, in our conduct, and in our gifts, Jesus will draw the world unto Him.

Let's give the world something to talk about by loving instead of hating, and respecting instead of disrespecting.

And he has made from one blood every nation of men to dwell on all the face of the earth (Acts 17:26a, NKJV).

Let's give the world something to talk about by transcending color, class, and distinction. We all come from one man, one blood, and we're all called to return to God from out of the sin that separated us.

To the black reader who wants to move onward, I ask you to pray this with me:

Father, I thank You for this revelation of my ancestral sins — sins of our fathers, which was also my sin. I confess the sin of idol worship that my fathers, my ancestors in Egypt, practiced. And I confess my sin. I confess my sin of intolerance. I confess my sins of resentment toward my white brother. I accept total responsibility.

I also ask You God to forgive us as a nation for our sins and heal us according to Your Word. Let the words of my mouth and the meditation of my heart be acceptable in Your sight, my Lord, my strength and my Redeemer. Amen.

To the white reader who wants to move onward, I ask you to pray this with me:

Father, help me to see my brother where he stands. Help me to draw nigh to him and to accept his difference and to make no difference out of the difference. Help me to fellowship with him under the banner of Jesus Christ, the Lord of lords and the King of kings, the great God of the universe.

Jesus, heal my irritated heart. Remove the racism that vexes my heart now. Father, help me see my brother where he stands that I might be drawn to him. Help me to come into fellowship with my brother in the truth and love of our mutual callings into your family and service. In Jesus' name, Amen.

Christianity transcends color. Therefore —

Put on the new man, which is renewed in knowledge after the image of him that created him: Where there is neither Greek nor Jew, circumcision nor uncircumcision, Barbarian, Scythian, bond nor free: but Christ in all, and in all (Col. 3:10-11).

ENDNOTES

CHAPTER THREE

[1] Herbert Lockyer, *All the Men of the Bible* (Grand Rapids, Mich.: Zondervan Publishing House, 1958), 134.
[2] M.C. Quattlebaum, *Niger Is Really Black* (Sarasota, Fla.: Lindsay Curtis Publishing Company, 1984), 23.
[3] Arthur W. Pink, *Gleanings in Genesis* (Chicago: The Moody Bible Institute, 1928), 124-5.
[4] Life Application [TM] Bible (Wheaton, Ill.: Tyndale House Publishers, 1988), note on Genesis 9:25.
[5] Pink, *Gleanings in Genesis*, 127.
[6] Matthew Henry, *Matthew Henry's Commentary on the Whole Bible* (Peabody, Mass.: Hendrickson Publishers, Inc., 1991), note on Genesis 9, verses 24-27, II, 1.
[7] Basil Davidson, *Africa in History* (New York: Macmillan Publishing Co., Inc., 1974), 21-22.
[8] Ibid.
[9] Lerone Bennett, Jr., *Before the Mayflower,* 5th rev. ed. (New York: Johnson Publishing Co., 1982), 7.

CHAPTER FOUR

[1] Chancellor Williams, *The Destruction of Black Civilization*, rev. ed. (Chicago: Third World Press, 1987), 18.
[2] H. L. Willmington, *Willmington's Guide to the Bible* (Wheaton, Ill.: Tyndale House Publishers, 1983), 193.
[3] Warren W. Wiersbe, *The Essential Everyday Bible Commentary* (Nashville, Tenn.: Thomas Nelson Publishers, 1993), margin note on Ex. 8:1-32.
[4] Willmington, *Guide*, 67.
[5] H. D. M. Spence and Joseph S. Exell, eds., *The Pulpit Commentary*, vol. 10, *Isaiah* (Grand Rapids, Mich.: Wm. B. Eerdmans Publishing Company, 1950), ch. XIX "Homilies by Various Authors," vv. 1-4, II.
[6] Joyce Andrews, *Bible Legacy of the Black Race* (Nashville, Tenn.: Winston-Derek Publishers, Inc., 1993), 196-197.
[7] Williams, *Black Civilization*, 59.
[8] Ibid., 178.
[9] Bennett, *Mayflower*, 10.

CHAPTER FIVE

[1] The New Scofield [R] Study Bible (Oxford University Press, Inc., 1967), introduction to the book of Judges.

CHAPTER SIX

[1] Jeffrey C. Stewart, *1001 Things Everyone Should Know About African American History* (New York: Doubleday, 1996), 10.
[2] Williams, *Black Civilization*, 240.
[3] Ibid., 256.
[4] Stewart, *1001 Things*, 15.
[5] Howard Smead, *The Afro-Americans* (New York: Chelsea House Publishers, 1989), 27.
[6] Stewart, *1001 Things*, 16.
[7] *Perseverance*, vol. 1 of *African Americans: Voices of Triumph*[TM] (Alexandria, Virg.: Time-Life Books, 1993), 46.
[8] John Hope Franklin and Alfred A. Moss, Jr., *From Slavery to Freedom* (New York: McGraw-Hill, Inc., 1988), 29.
[9] *Perseverance*, 43.
[10] Ibid., 32.

CHAPTER SEVEN

[1] Andrews, *Bible Legacy*, xiii-xiv.
[2] U.S. Department of Justice, Bureau of Justice Statistics, "State and Federal Prisons Report Record Growth During Last 12 Months," press release, 3 December 1995.
[3] Ibid., "One-Quarter of the Crime Victims Who Are Shot Are Young Black Males," press release, 11 April 1996.
[4] Stewart, *1001 Things*, 31.
[5] "Rival Rappers' Deaths Spark Fear of Fighting," *The Orlando Sentinel*, 11 March 1997, sec. A.
[6] Henry, *Commentary*, note on Isaiah 19, verses 1-17, III.

CHAPTER NINE

[1] David Jackson, "Ascent and Grandeur," *Chicago Tribune*, March 15, 1995 in Dinesh D'Souza, *The End of Racism* (New York: The Free Press, 1995), 428.
[2] E. Stanley Jones, *The Way* (Garden City, N.Y.:Doubleday & Company, Inc., 1978), 119.

[3] Carla Power and Allison Samuels, "Battling for Souls," *Newsweek*, 30 October 1995, 46-47.
[4] Ibid.
[5] Dinesh D'Souza, *The End of Racism* (New York: The Free Press, 1995), 428.
[6] Ibid.
[7] Ibid., 429.
[8] Interview by Morley Safer, *60 Minutes*, CBS News, 24 November 1996.

CHAPTER TEN
[1] Rosie Milligan, *Satisfying the Black Man Sexually* (Los Angeles: Professional Business Consultants, 1994), 41.
[2] Ibid.
[3] Jackie Fowler, *My People* (Tulsa, Okla.: Fowler Enterprises, 1991), 9.
[4] Aubrey Andelin, *Man of Steel and Velvet* (Pierce City, Mo.: Pacific Press Santa Barbara, 1972), 11-13.

CHAPTER ELEVEN
[1] Williams, *Black Civilization*, 246-247.
[2] Stewart, *1001 Things*, 10.
[3] Ibid., 123.
[4] Ibid., 124.
[5] Ibid.
[6] Ellis Cose, "One Drop of Bloody History," *Newsweek*, 13 February 1995, 70.
[7] "Boy Emerging From Coma After Beating in Chicago," *The Orlando Sentinel*, 30 March 1997, Sec. A.
[8] Jolie Solomon, "Texaco's Troubles," *Newsweek*, 25 November 1996, 48-50.
[9] Marc Levinson, "Always Open to Its Customers?" *Newsweek*, 19 July 1993, 36.

CHAPTER THIRTEEN
[1] "Wall Busting 101," *New Man*, September 1996, 36-39.

CHAPTER FOURTEEN
[1] Nathan McCall, *Makes Me Wanna Holler* (New York: Vintage Books, 1994), 55.

CHAPTER FIFTEEN
[1] Raymond M. Corbin, *1999 Facts About Blacks* (Providence, R.I.: Beckham House Publishers, Inc., 1986), 5, 180.
[2] Bennett, *Mayflower,* 641.
[3] Gloria Busch Johnson and Robert Funk, "Beyond the Protests," *Guideposts*, February 1997, 9-14.

SUGGESTED READING

Andrews, Joyce. *Bible Legacy of the Black Race*. Nashville, Tenn.: Winston-Derek Publishers, 1993.

Bennett, Lerone, Jr. *Before the Mayflower*. 5th rev. ed. New York: Johnson Publishing Co., 1962.

Davidson, Basil. *Africa in History*. New York: Macmillan Publishing Co. Inc., 1974.

Fowler, Jackie. *My People*. Tulsa, Okla.: Fowler Enterprises, 1991.

Johnson, John L. *The Black Biblical Heritage*. 1975. Reprint, Nashville, Tenn.: Winston-Derek Publishers Inc., 1993.

Lockyer, Herbert. *All the Men of the Bible*. Grand Rapids, Mich.: Zondervan Publishing House, 1958.

McCall, Nathan. *Makes Me Wanna Holler*. New York: Vintage Books, 1994.

Milligan, Rosie. *Satisfying the Black Man Sexually*. Los Angeles: Professional Business Consultants, 1994.

Pink, Arthur W. *Gleanings in Genesis*. Chicago: Moody Press, 1981.

Stewart, Jeffrey C. *1001 Things Everyone Should Know About African American History*. New York: Doubleday, 1996.

Williams, Chancellor. *The Destruction of Black Civilization*. Rev. ed. Chicago: Third World Press, 1987.

Windsor, Rudolph R. *From Babylon to Timbuktu*. Rev. ed. 1969. Reprint, Atlanta: Windsor's Golden Series, 1988.